THE

MEDLEY

OF

MAST AND SAIL

A view from Whitby Station.
The barquentine is but a memory: the gas lamps are gone and
the dock is now a car park!

THE
MEDLEY
OF
MAST AND SAIL

A CAMERA RECORD

407 photographic illustrations of many of the world's vanished sailing
craft, both great and small, accompanied by comment and description
by Frank G. G. Carr, Richard M. Cookson, Alex. Hurst,
Michael K. Stammers and others.

WITH AN INTRODUCTION
BY
FRANK G. G. CARR

NAVAL INSTITUTE PRESS

Published and distributed in the United States of America by the Naval
Institute Press

Library of Congress Catalog Card No. 76-62879

ISBN 0-87021-939-1

Printed in Great Britain

CONTENTS

Norwegian brig ORNEN of 1866 flaunts her stun'sails.

PUBLISHERS' NOTE

It is easy to speak of the Age of Sail and to have in mind merely the famous clippers or big sailing ships which have appeared in books of one sort or another or, alternatively, to consider that period in terms of the various forms of types and rigs which existed.

The point which is so often overlooked is the fantastically vast number of ships, both great and small, which were afloat in trade and going about their business all over the world. The majority of them never hit the headlines and were simply taken for granted as part of the scene. Indeed, several pictures in this book which show a vessel passing out of port under all sail demonstrate how the bystanders were all looking the other way, whereas such a thing today would be regarded as a major event!

It is possible to produce a single book of large dimensions on almost every type of sailing craft, or on every nation or on every ship-owner. This volume is presented rather as a photograph album of the sailing scene laying, as in all albums, more emphasis on one feature or another than on others. Many of the ships are little known: others achieved considerable fame. Each and all had their own characters and a certain fascination.

Because this collection of pictures is presented as an album, it is not sub-divided into specific sections. Were it a definitive history, it might have been logical to have dealt, perhaps, with wooden square-riggers and to have followed then with their steel successors, or to have confined barges, in their various forms, to one chapter. There are no chapters, because these vessels all rubbed shoulders together.

VII

A Thames barge would load alongside a full-rigger; Mersey flats were in their tideway along with the schooners and deep-watermen and a brig would tow out of harbour astern of her tug with several fishermen. There were no class distinctions between types of vessels in the days of sail, and thus there are none in this book.

Like the ships portrayed, the book permits itself the odd excursion into other realms and into other seas. It does not pretend to be comprehensive in this, the first such volume, but we believe that the pictures, together with the accompanying texts, may provide some insight into many aspects of that lately departed age of "Sticks and String" which are often overlooked. Indeed, certain omissions are intentional, since the object of the book is to record the humdrum rather than the famous vessels, though some of the latter are included as a matter of balance. Some of the photographs are very old.

Some people think that certain of the famous clippers represented the perfection of the sailing ship. Others might favour the last big, powerful four-masters. Perhaps the most likely aspirant for this title might be the Gloucester schooners built to work the Grand banks and George's Bank. They were fast: they were efficient; they were beautiful to behold and, above all, they were eminently "able", to use the Gloucesterman's own adjective for them. Having made that case, their omission from this book may seem to be remarkable. They are not included because they have good coverage in another book which we shall be publishing, and we are loath to commit the sin of repetition! Yet they are in good company. Whole sea-faring nations; important trades and the bulk of the infinite variety of rigs and types must, of necessity, be reserved for future volumes. The potential is too enormous to be covered in one book.

Sailing ships did not spend all their time in calendar-like glory dipping through sunny seas with gleaming canvas, any more than they were constantly embattled with fearsome storms. Much of their time was spent in port. Some probably spent more than half their careers in harbour, and it was certainly in and around the land that they were chiefly to be seen. That is the stark truth of it, and thus the balance of this book in which the continuity is based on location or consequence rather than on type or rig.

LIST OF ILLUSTRATIONS

XI

XII

ACKNOWLEDGEMENTS

THIS BOOK, which has been long on the stocks, has been very much a co-operative effort, and the Publishers wish to thank all those who have assisted in its compilation. First and foremost, our thanks are due to Mr. Frank G. G. Carr, not only for his written commentaries on pages 25-33, 77-92, 140-156 and 284-289, but for writing the Introduction and for his unfailing help and assistance in the selection of pictures and for all the advice and experience which he has brought to bear so willingly. We are also grateful to Mr. Michael Stammers, who has written the comments on the Trows of the Bristol Channel and the Mersey Flats, besides advising on matters pertaining to Merseyside.

It is pleasant to record that some of those who have provided essential information in this volume have got in touch with us and established friendly relationships as a result of reading our previous books. Regrettably, there are limits to the content of a single volume, and not all that has been contributed has been included in this one, but we wish to acknowledge in particular the information received from Mr. A. B. Andersen, Director of the Stavanger Sjøfartsmuseum: Cdr. Peter Davies of Mylor, who corrected a case of mistaken identity: Capt. Jim Gaby of Sydney, N.S.W.: Mr. K. G. Holm of Varberg: Capt. Archie Horka of New Jersey: Capt. G. Paterson of Brighton: Monsieur Henri Picard of Royan: Capt. K. A. Thoresen of Maarnesstrand, and Capt. Frank Walker of Hattiesville, Miss. Our thanks are due, also, to Mr. George Osbon and Mr. Denis Stonham of the National Maritime Museum for their assistance in identification and verification of both ships and places, and to the former for the information incorporated on page 231, while much of the written material has been edited by Mr. Alex. Hurst and Mr. R. M. Cookson, who have both also made direct contributions to the commentaries.

There has been no less co-operation in the matter of the photographs, although, where negatives have changed hands or been placed at the disposal of more than one agency, the quotation of sources must necessarily be somewhat arbitrary in some instances. Ten were by Adamson of Rothesay: No. 101 from Mr. John Allendale through the good offices of Mr. Walter Dowsett: seven came from the late Daniel R. Bolt. Both Mr. Frank Carr and Mr. Richard Cookson have delved extensively into their collections: No. 316 was by Mr. John Dubas of Baltimore: No. 218 by Messrs. Gibson of Penzance: four by the late Mr. F. C. Gould of Gravesend: Some 22 from the late Cdr. H. O. Hill: 26 from Alex. A. Hurst, in addition to the two endpapers: Four from Mr. Basil Fielden, taken by Mr. H. N. Cooper: No. 373 from the Keystone News Agency: Nos. 66/73 and 76 from the late Capt. A. C. Matzelaar: No. 233 from the late Capt. T. D. Manning: No. 138 from the Morton Waters Co. of San Francisco: Four by Opie's of Falmouth: No. 208 from Messrs. Paull of Redruth: No. 357 from the Peabody Museum, Salem: Several by Priestley and Son of Wallasey: No. 87

by Portsmouth Newspapers: Two from the late James Randall: No. 382 from the San Francisco Maritime Museum (W. A. Scott coll.): The Frontispiece and Nos. 9-12, 14 and 404 from the Sutcliffe Galleries, Whitby: 156 and 158/9 by Mr. R. C. Shepherd: No. 162 by the late Capt. Sam Svensson: No. 367 by the Sydney Morning News and Nos. 377-9 from Capt. K. A. Thoresen of Maarnesstrand.

For the rest, most have come either from the extensive collection of the late Capt. F. C. Poyser who, from world-wide sources, created the Nautical Photo Agency, most (but not all) of which is now in the National Maritime Museum at Greenwich, and from the Northern Publishing Co. The latter included such photographers as Cooper of Liverpool and Barnard of Hull and several of those already listed, while Capt. Poyser's pictures included many people well-known in nautical circles, some of whom have already been detailed. Others in this category, included in both Mr. Carr's and Mr. Cookson's collections include:—the late Mr. F. N. Adams: Capt. Adam: Amos of Dover: C. H. Berrison: the late R. Stuart Bruce: the late Capt. W. H. Colbeck: Miss Alice Cocks: Mr. R. W. C. Courtney: de Maus of Port Chalmers: Monsieur P. de Meslon: Miss Hay: Mr. J. Henderson, Mr. le Good: Capt. Morrison: Mr. G. Payne: Capt. Pettigrew: the late Mr. W. A. Sharman: W. A. Swadley: Mr. F. T. Wayne and Mr. York. Indeed, it is difficult to discriminate between all the sources due to duplication. At one time, for instance, all Mr. James Randall's, Cdr. H. O. Hill's and Mr. Alex. Hurst's pictures were in Capt. Poyser's collection. Thus we have listed *our* sources.

Once again, we thank all those who have helped in this book. We regret that some are no longer with us to see the final fruits, and we also hope that, being so vast a subject, we shall be enabled to follow this one with further volumes. We only publish a limited number of books, and then only those which we deem to merit publication. We are not in any commercial "rat-race" and take a more old-fashioned attitude to our operations. Since we cannot afford to do otherwise, we must make our books pay for themselves, but much of our reward lies in the correspondence, contacts and many friendships which have been formed as a result of our efforts. Lest anyone shrinks from writing to a publisher about his own nautical interests, we ask that such diffidence be cast aside and that, if any readers feel that they have excellent pictures of some lesser known aspect of sail, or information which they would like to share with the world, we should be happy to hear from them. The field of local craft throughout the world—or, indeed, of sailing craft of all sorts—is a huge and complex one, upon which no one man is competent to speak!

INTRODUCTION

"Ships and the sea; there's nothing finer made". Thus spoke the Dauber in John Masefield's classic poem about the artist who so loved ships that he went to sea as a foc's'le hand in order to paint them as they really were. "There is so much to learn" he said, "with sails and ropes, and how the sails look, full or being furled." He might have added that the sea, with oceans and estuaries bordering an almost infinite variety of continents and islands, has over the centuries produced a fascinating medley of craft of innumerable shapes, rigs and sizes, evolved by the genius of man to suit their local needs. To offer a selection from that medley, as seen by the camera, is the object of this book.

Fortunately, man's instinct to make pictures of things with which he is familiar has given us, where ships and smaller craft are concerned, a rich heritage of pictorial representation stretching from the primitive rock carvings of the Neolithic age to the latest creations of the 35 mm reflex camera. Equally fortunate is the fact that the sailing ship is essentially such a thing of beauty that she inevitably inspires a desire to record her. Thus it is no mere chance that the subject of one of the earliest photographs ever taken in this country should have been Brunel's *Great Britain* fitting out at Bristol in 1843, the year in which she was built. This really superb record, unbelievably clear in its detail, was secured by Fox Talbot, the English gentleman who devised independently his own system of photography, and only four years earlier had succeeded in producing the world's first photographic negative.

There is an object lesson in this, for it shows that no-one wishing to take maritime photographs should be deterred by lack of expensive equipment. It cannot be too strongly emphasised that some of the finest pictures have been obtained with the simplest apparatus, for the merit and quality of a photograph depend far more on the artistry and skill of the man behind the lens than on the extent of his gadgetry. Before the first World War, the late J. P. Hodge secured some of the most delightful pictures of local types of craft, including the bawley *Ethel* in Plate 118, using a small box-and-bellows camera of late-Victorian vintage embellished with 'do-it-yourself' improvements that could hardly have been bettered by the great Heath Robinson himself.

Most remarkable of all were the hundreds of photographs taken by that astonishing Gravesend photographer, F. C. Gould, around the turn of the century, including his magnificent series of racing barges. The *Haughty Belle* in Plate 100 is one of them. Using an enormous camera, loaded with a 12 x 10 inch glass plate and *hand held*, for his moving subjects ruled out the aid of a tripod, he would charter a waterman's wherry and, out in the river, wait for his prey to approach until it was near enough to fill the desired area in his home-made wire-framed open view-finder. With both hands needed to hold and aim the camera, he had none left free to work the shutter. This difficulty he overcame, however, by mounting the bulb for its remote control within two hinged wooden clap-boards held between his teeth. When the right moment arrived, with one hard bite the exposure was made: a snapshot in every sense of the word!

Let it not be imagined, however, that artistic merit has been the deciding factor in selecting photographs for this book. That would have been far too limiting. Sea pictures differ greatly in quality, as is inevitable when they have to be taken in such widely varying conditions. One cannot command studio lighting at sea in a gale of wind. The criterion has been the intrinsic maritime significance of the subject as illustrating the trends of hull and rig in the saga of commercial sail. Better an indifferent photograph of a stackie barge under weigh than no photograph of her at all; and that principle has been applied throughout this collection. It is the only practicable way to produce a representative assortment.

But enough of the Prologue—the Play's the thing! Ringing up the curtain, we present the Medley of Mast and Sail—a Camera Record:—

Frank G. G. Carr

Barge-yacht VENTA in the Wallet.

XXI

1. SUSSEX MAID.

The sea showed an unsurpassed splendour,
    While the wind, in each force of its scale,
Made music no *maestro* could render
    To match the medley of mast and sail'.
                        (From 'Sails of the Sea'.)

2. Four-masted barque CRAIGERNE rounding the Horn.

XXII

3.

Victorian and Edwardian artists are sometimes thought to have allowed themselves a good deal of licence in the number of craft in their paintings of coastal scenes. They seldom exaggerated. Craft were smaller and there were, literally, thousands of them. They were not confined to the big and famous ports, but to be found loading and discharging in tiny places and on the beaches themselves. Small though they were, many voyaged to the ends of the earth and, in their day, the barques and full-riggers amongst them were considered to be large and staunch vessels. Few appeared in the history books and they were so much a part of the scene that they were taken for granted and, in consequence, the majority passed into oblivion. There are more vessels in this view from Plymouth than appear at first glance. There is an anchored barque in the left distance, and the brigantines and schooners, with the bigger brigs, were the work-horses of their age before the railways and, later, heavy lorries took their hold on world transport.

1

4. Brig flying light with a fair wind.

With two masts, square-rigged on each, the brig was one of the commonest rigs to be found in Europe and elsewhere. Few people who have grown up since the outbreak of the First World War have ever seen one, but it was not many years before that when the seas and ports were full of them, many trading all over the world. They seemed to vanish from the face of the seas almost faster than any other type, as though some malevolent sea-god had waved his wand.

The *Aid*, of Åbo, seen opposite, is seen wearing the old Russian ensign before the revolution and before Finland, in which Åbo is an important port, had achieved its independence. She was a fairly typical vessel, of 291 tons N.R.T., built at Thoraswarf in 1873 and owned by Lindberg of Nagen in 1888 when this picture was taken.

There were, of course, many fine-lined, clipper brigs, but many appeared somewhat tubby in their hull form. Nevertheless, they made their voyages with amazing regularity.

5. *The Russian brig AID, of Åbo.*

6. Snow CELERITY towing in to port.

Despite the smoke of the well-known Lowestoft paddle tug *Imperial*, it is easy to see that the wooden brig in tow of her on the opposite page is smartly kept. Her sails are beautifully stowed (though the fore topgallantsail is not bent), and she is loosing off her topsails, whilst her jibbom is still rigged in. Unusually, she is being towed on a bridle. Astern we see the masts of the fishing fleet lying in harbour with the odd coastal ketch.

4

7.   *Brig towing out of Lowestoft.*

8. Snow CELERITY ashore.

One of the great trades for the brigs was the carriage of coal from the North-East coast to ports and beaches all round England and to the Baltic. Many were owned in the Durham and Northumberland ports, but the *Celerity*, which became well-known for years on the east coast, was built in 1867 at Middlesborough by R. Craggs & Sons and owned at Lowestoft, by J. S. Sterry, a local coal merchant, of the port, to which she traded for years. Rigged as a snow, she registered 215 tons, being 103.3 feet in length. She is also shown in Plate 6 on page 4. The carriage of coal was not by any means confined to vessels rigged as brigs and snows.

9. *OPAL drying sails in Whitby. (Note the many cobles in these Whitby pictures. Although they have developed twin skids each side of the keel, these small craft, some 20 feet long, are of direct lineage from the Norse and the Danelaw. See pp. 306/12.)*

10. Brig OPAL sending down her topgallant-masts.

The brig *Opal* of 154 tons was built in 1845 in Greenock, and was fairly typical of the collier brigs, being at this time owned by G. Hopper of Whitby. Bentinck booms were common, as in these pictures, and avoided working sheets and tacks, although braces were led forward to the bowsprit and it hauled up to the yard, so that the sail was furled like an upper topsail. The East coast and the approaches to the Thames were often full of these craft which bore most of the country's coal. Flying kites may be associated with the clippers, but very many of these craft carried stunsails, and the irons can be seen in the barquentine which forms the frontispiece.*

The schooner *Alert* had been built in 1802 at Whitby and when the picture was taken was owned by John Danby of W. Hartlepool, while the ketch *Sara* was of 68 tons and built in Hull in 1899.

*See p. VI.

8

11. *Scene in Whitby—a brigantine, ketch and barque on the mud.*

12. *ASTRAEA (foreground) in Whitby. Southampton brigs beyond. The ASTRAEA was then owned by Walter (later Lord) Runciman, whose shipping interests became so enormous. He had bought her from W. W. Pilkington of St. Helen's.*

13.   Wreck of brig LILY.

A difficulty arising from the multiplicity of craft in the nineteenth century lies in the number of the same size and name. This *Lily* is believed to be one built in Montrose in 1867 and owned by G. Largie & Co. of that port. She was 235 tons, measuring 105.1 x 25.3 x 14.4 ft. A 160-ton Liverpool brig of this name, bound from Liverpool towards Ambrejo in West Africa with a mixed cargo including cloth, rum and 40 tons of gun-powder, was driven back from a position off Queenstown up the Irish Sea and finally cast ashore by the tide in the Sound of the Calf of Man, some men being lost.

Lloyds agent took possession of the wreck, since the Manxmen, intent on plunder, had to be kept off with firearms. Next morning, December 30th, 1853, the gunpowder blew up, blowing thirty people to pieces. The blast was so great that candles were blown out and one man knocked over by the shock in a mine three miles away!

14.   The Whitby skyline is the same as the frontispiece. The schooner ALERT on the right was built as a sloop. The schooner LIVELY is on the left ahead of the ketch SARA, while the brig beyond her is the HOPEWELL. Some cobles are setting sail.

15. *Brigantine ABEJA.*

Generally a little smaller than a brig, the brigantine was an attractive
craft, being square-rigged on her fore and fore-and-aft on her main.
The *Abeja* is seen towing into Littlehampton on the only occasion she
ever visited the port after she was built there in 1881 by J. & W. B.
Harvey for Spanish owners. Later she was bought back to the British
flag, but was sunk by the Germans in the 1914-18 war.

Opposite, we see another brigantine drying her sails in Lowestoft
in 1888. Across the basin lies another, astern of a barque, probably
Scandinavian with her windmill pump and very likely built in one of
the Canadian Maritime Provinces. Astern of the nearest brigantine is
a ketch. These smaller craft often kept the same crews together for
long periods, and their men tended to be more stable, with more home
contacts, than their deep-water counter-parts which, in any case, paid
off their men in port, when they soon became scattered.

16. *Brigantine drying her sails in Lowestoft in 1888.*

17. WILLIAM DYER.

Built in 1865 by Lumsden of Sunderland for F. French, the *William Dyer* was owned in Guernsey and measured 97.9 x 23.6 x 13.3 ft., being 186 tons gross. In these two pictures she is seen leaving Littlehampton. In these days, no doubt, the quay would be filled with jostling people, interested in sailing ships or not, to view such a sight, but apart from a man with his bicycle in the top picture, she is passing out unnoticed, since the two figures in the larger picture are looking the other way. Usually sailing craft were towed in and out the long narrow entrance to the harbour by the old paddle-tug *Jumna*, but the *William Dyer* has the wind right aft and is making her way to sea without help from anybody and without any towage bill! There is no panic station: it is all part of the daily round, and a far cry from the crowded decks of such little 'training' and adventure ships which are occasionally seen today.

14

18. *WILLIAM DYER leaving Littlehampton.*

19. Brigantine making sail.

Littlehampton was by no means the only place where such close navigation could be observed. Opposite we see the Norwegian barquentine *Alfred Gibbs* in the canal at Moss, in Norway. Originally built as a barque in 1851 by Wood and Sons, of Bath, Maine, she was by this time owned in Christianssand by J. Lange, and was of 387 tons.

Above is a typical British brigantine making sail outside Littlehampton. A man is aloft loosing off the topgallantsail, while the rest of the hands hoist her mainsail. Like the *William Dyer* and many others, she is setting a square-knocked staysail.

16

20.   *ALFRED GIBBS, bow view.*

21.   *ALFRED GIBBS, quarter view.*

22. Brigantine VIVID, of 1852.

The *Vivid* has a different appearance altogether with the almost piratical rake to her masts. She is of an earlier vintage, having been built at Rye—formerly one of the Cinque ports—in 1851. She was of 162 tons and measured 91.4 x 23.9 x 13.3 ft., being owned by F. C. Clothier at Faversham, on the Kentish Swale.

The Registers for 1888, when Plate 23 was taken, show no less than eighty-four sailing vessels named *Anna*, of which fourteen were brigantines of much the same size! This *Anna* was a Dane, the picture appearing to be the more dramatic since she has been picked up water-logged and is here seen being towed into Great Yarmouth by the famous old paddle-tug *United Service*, which accomplished a good deal of salvage work in her time. (See page 30.)

The *Anna* was probably loaded with timber, which was, of course, the one cargo that was salvation to a water-logged vessel and would keep her afloat in some sort almost indefinitely. Once such a vessel was abandoned at sea, she became a floating menace to navigation.

18

23. *The water-logged Danish brigantine ANNA being towed into Yarmouth by the tug UNITED SERVICE in 1888.*

24. Brigantine GUITAR.

Close-hauled, this jaunty little brigantine with her jibboom and flush deck is an attractive sight as she sails close up by the wind. Typical enough of hundreds like her, she might be found running round our own coasts; to the Baltic, anywhere along the Atlantic coasts, or to the Mediterranean. Oddly, there was little interchange of men, on the whole, between the short-sea traders and the deep-watermen.

Opposite, looking out along the Lowestoft harbour entrance, are two scenes repeated constantly in the last century. Aesthetic appeal, afloat or ashore, has given way to dubious efficiency.

25. *Old-timer passing the Isle of Wight. (Needles on the right.)*

26. *Lowestoft harbour entrance—smack-rigged fifie ahead.*

28. *Typical dock scenes of the last century. The schooner ELFRIDA lies alongside an unknown barque with her jibboom rigged in. (Note her unusual billboard.) The two barques with their upper yards sent down are probably laid up.*

29. *The last brigantine to leave Lowestoft in 1928 . . .*

30. *. . . was not so unlike the VIDFARNE, seen in Lowestoft in 1877, half a century earlier.*

31. Ketch-rigged Yarmouth Drifter HARRY, YH 857.

The drift net fishing of Great Yarmouth is of very ancient origin, governed by statutes and regulations far back into medieval times, that of Lowestoft being of much more recent date. For the first seven decades of the nineteenth century, the fishing was carried on by three-masted luggers of some 46 ft. in overall length, fully decked, and manned by a crew of ten. In about 1870, the middle mast was removed, leaving a dipping lug foresail on a mast stepped very far forward, and a standing lug mizzen carried on a mast generally taller than the foremast, and raking well forward. This sail was sheeted to a long spar extending well out over the counter and steeved sharply upwards to keep it clear of the sea when pitching. The appearance

25

32. Drifters using sweeps — 'wooden tops'ls' — in Lowestoft.

was precisely that of the counter-sterned Penzance lugger 55 PZ seen in Plate 197; a craft in fact copied closely from the East Coast type and unusual in Cornwall. The foremast was stepped in a tabernacle and made to lower into a crutch or 'mitchboard' when riding to the nets, and the deck was thus kept well clear of obstructions to allow plenty of space for handling the nets when hauled. Between the mitchboard and the mizzen mast was the capstan, fitted with bars, round which the crew would trudge when hauling in the nets, often extending upwards of a mile away from the drifter.

There were three distinct seasons for the herring fishing, known as the spring, the midsummer and the Michaelmas or autumn fisheries; and in the mid-eighteen seventies it became the practice to equip some of the drifters with ketch rig and to use them for trawling in the off seasons. At first the same masts were used, but the foremast

26

33. Small 'long-boomer' — Yarmouth trawler SULTAN, c.1895.

was rigged with a tall loose-footed gaff sail together with a narrow fore staysail in place of the old dipping lug. It was then discovered that these ketch-rigged craft, or 'dandies', were so much handier under sail, although not so fast as those with the original lug rig, that the change became permanent. Through the innate conservatism of the fishermen, however, they were still called 'luggers' in spite of the changed rig. In later craft, when the earlier dual-purpose masts were no longer carried, the foremast was made longer, and the appearance became more what one is accustomed to in a ketch. The Yarmouth drifter *Harry*, in Plate 31 is a typical example.

Steam capstans by Elliott & Garood, of Beccles, were fitted from 1884 onwards. In these, two horizontal cylinders mounted on the bed-plate were supplied with steam through the hollow shaft on which the barrel rotated.*

*Note: The first lugger to be so provided was the *BEACONSFIELD*.

27

34. Yarmouth tug REAPER towing trawlers to sea from Gorleston.

By 1902, no fewer than 230 luggers of the type seen in Plate 34 were fishing from Lowestoft, at which time there were only 10 steam drifters in the port. Yet so rapid was their demise that not one sailing drifter remained after the First World War.

Trawling began from Yarmouth in the early 1840's with the arrival of smacks from Barking. The early vessels were cutter-rigged and known as 'long-boomers'. An example is the 49-ton *Sultan*, YH 728, of 1866, seen in Plate 33, which is almost identical with an oil painting dated October 1899 in the Yarmouth Museums. She is similar in hull, although not in rig, to a model of the long-boomer *Yarborough* in the same collection. Later these craft were rigged as ketches, and a number of them appear in Plate 34 being towed to sea from Gorleston by the clinker-built wooden paddle-tug *Reaper*, launched at South Shields for a Sunderland owner and eventually sunk in collision with the Yarmouth tug *Advance* in 1901. The most famous tug at Yarmouth, however, was the *United Service*, seen in

28

35. Paddle tug UNITED SERVICE with Scots fishing craft (two fifies and a zulu) plus the Yarmouth trawler CLUPIDE in tow.

36. A Lowestoft trawler comes home.

Plates 23 and 35 where she is towing in a mixed bag of three Scottish fishing boats, namely: two fifies and a zulu, and one Yarmouth sailing trawler. Built at South Shields in 1871, this clinker-built wooden vessel, with a single-cylinder engine of 44 R.H.P., continued working until she was broken up in 1942. In summer she used to carry trippers and eventually acquired the distinction of being the last vessel ever to run a passenger service to Cromer.

The Lowestoft trawlers, Plates 36 and 37, were far more numerous than those of Yarmouth, and in the nineties caused Lowestoft to rank as the second fishing port of the Kingdom. The industry here began much later than at Yarmouth, and it was not until 1860 that extensive trawling was started by smacks from

37. *By 1930, when this picture was taken, the death knell of the Lowestoft trawlers had already tolled.*

Ramsgate. These in turn had originally appeared there from Brixham to begin trawling from the Thanet port in about 1823. In later years, Ramsgate smacks, not quite as large as the bigger ones of Lowestoft and Brixham, were generally known as 'toshers', and a typical Ramsgate tosher, the *Idea*, is seen in the foreground in Plate 38, from a photograph taken in the 1890's.

In addition to the deep-watermen, there were smaller craft which trawled in the Would, the waterway that lies between the Haisborough Sand and the shore and, although these varied individually in type, they were generally referred to collectively as 'Wolders'. What may fairly be regarded as a representative example forms the subject of Plate 39. This shows LT 395, the *Samuel and Ellen*, a

31

38. The Dock at Ramsgate in the 1890's, with two 'toshers' and square-riggers.

clinker-built transom-sterned cutter with a crew of three. She carried a trawl too big for a shrimper and too small for deep-water fishing. In 1896 she was owned by D. Coleman of Lowestoft.

32

39. *SAMUEL AND ELLEN, LT 395, proceeding to sea from Gorleston.*

40. PORTHISCALE

In the days of wooden ship-building, vessels were being built almost all round the coasts in many small ports and creeks which are seldom associated with that activity today. Shoreham, in Sussex, was a flourishing port in the nineteenth century, building vessels and owning fleets which circumnavigated the globe, their house-flags being seen as far away as New Zealand. The vessel shown above, the *Porthiscale*, was built there in 1866 by Shuttleworth's for Seymour of Liverpool, being a wooden vessel with iron beams of 453 tons.

By 1883 she had passed to S. T. Tandevin of Guernsey, and is believed to have come under Scandinavian ownership later on. This is a fair inference from the windmill pump which may be seen in the picture. These extremely sensible devices never seem to have been adopted by British vessels and were considered to be a Scandinavian foible, though some American wooden vessels did carry them too.

41. Oslo Harbour — BEREAN in the centre.

Pumping was soul-killing and back-breaking work which the wind did free with those windmills!

The *Berean*, seen above, was a smart little barque of 562 tons nett built in 1869 by Pile of Sunderland for Capt. Walker, whose ships were managed by Messrs. Devitt & Moore, in whose office Walker had a room. Originally crossing three skysails, she was beautifully finished, even the lining of her foc's'le being of teak, while her poop was laid with Kauri pine without a single knot in it. After 18 years, when she was re-metalled, she had never been re-caulked since building, and she never was, even when, as in this picture, carrying ice under the Norwegian flag in her old age. In her prime she made fast passages on the Tasmanian and Brisbane runs, but was condemned when damaged after being struck by the Danzig s.s. *Julia* in clear weather off Gravesend in April 1910. Such vessels did not need pumps!

35

42. Wooden ship being broken up in Portugal.

This picture gives a general idea of the construction of a wooden vessel being dismantled. Ships built of oak or teak could last almost indefinitely, whereas soft-wood ones tended to become crank after about ten years of life. The wooden ship would generally perform better than iron or steel ones in light weather, but in hard weather the position was generally reversed. Moreover, the immense amount of timber used in the construction of a wooden vessel rendered her hull heavier than a comparable iron or steel ship. In the event of stranding or fire, the wooden vessel was obviously at a greater disadvantage and, with the exception of such superb examples as the *Berean*, the majority faced the spectre of intermittent pumping. The reluctance to equip them with windmill pumps in so many countries was but one aspect of the innate conservatism which seems to have gripped both owners and ship-masters alike.

36

43. VARDÖEN.

A few shipmasters experimented with perforated sails, which were instituted by an Italian ship-master. It was shown that vessels so fitted not only sailed faster by releasing a cushion of dead wind on the after side of the sails, but that their canvas was much easier to stow in bad weather, since it did not 'balloon' to the same degree. Indeed, some yachts followed the principle between the wars, particularly in their spinnakers and balloon jibs. Few masters adopted this principle, but it is well known that the captains of the *Cimba* and *Loch Torridon*, to mention but two, did use the perforations, and it was another example of reluctance to adopt change. However, more ships did use perforated sails than is commonly supposed, and here we see the *Vardöen*, a common-or-garden Norwegian barque which, built at Risor in 1893, had several Norwegian owners. Later named *Victoria*, she was wrecked on the coast of Cuba in 1921.

37

44. ESTER.

As a rule, it was only those ships in the first-class in which a perfection in fittings and looks were striven for, and the vast majority of sailing ships sailing the seas, of whatever degree, were designed to be profitable work-horses. Most sailing craft, of any rig, have a certain attraction, whether under **sail or** not, and there were infinite variations, even amongst the square-**riggers**. The *Ester*, seen above towing out in ballast, was built in Grimstad in 1886 and was flushed-decked forward. After having four owners in that port she was sold to Australia in 1910 and registered in Hobart in 1912.

Opposite, the *Harold*, towing in with a heavy list, was built as the *Annie M. Law* of Yarmouth, Nova Scotia, for the famous Canadian Law fleet, being of 1179 tons and constructed at Argyle, in that province. Later she became Norwegian. Few people realise the immense number of sailing craft built in the Maritime provinces, both square-rigged and fore-and-aft. F. W. Wallace has listed 3700 of over 500 tons, and the numbers below this figure were legion, almost all being built between 1840 and 1920.

45. Norwegian ship HAROLD, ex ANNIE M. LAW, towing into port with a heavy list.

46. *ALA off the Humber estuary.*

Reading the histories of the famous sailing ships, it is easy to forget that the bulk of the cargoes were carried by craft like the *Ellen*, built at Grimstad in 1893 of 513 tons. Note how her sails, clewed up to the quarters of the yards, look when being loosed. The *Ala*, of Drammen, was built in Åbo in Finland in 1867 while the *Eliezer*, seen here running out of the Clyde, was built in Krageroe in 1884 and, after having several Norwegian owners, stranded on Vlisland when bound to Cardiff from Kristianssand with pit-props under Thorkild Stray's house-flag. The *Asta*, of 511 tons and built at Drammen, is seen here sailing down Gravesend Reach and passing a local bawley. These vessels are all Norwegian, but similar ones were to be found under all flags. (See page VII.)

40

47. The Norwegian barque ELLEN towing out to sea.

48. ELIEZER.

49. ASTA.

50. THE MURRAY.

The Murray is shown here still in the hands of her builders, Halls of Aberdeen, in 1861. Of 902 tons, she was the last wooden clipper built for Anderson's Orient Line, being kept in the Adelaide trade with cargo and passengers. Whilst this ship is high in the water, which never enhances a ship's appearance, it nevertheless poses the question whether the clippers really were of such superlative appearance. Of course, their under-water lines were a joy, but the single topsails (seen here), and their rather rakish rig, so common in the famous American clippers of the fifties, give them rather the look of a greyhound (which is apt enough) as compared with the labrador retriever of the medium clippers which followed them. However, appearance was a mere by-product of a ship's design!

43

51. MORNING LIGHT.

This vessel, seen approaching Moss, must not be confused with another *Morning Light* built in 1855 as an Australian packet, which, at 2377 tons, was the biggest vessel built in St. Johns and later the German *J. M. Wendt.* This *Morning Light* of 1327 tons, was built at Meteghan, N.S., passed from the Canadian flag to the Norwegians in 1891, being owned in Oslo, and was sold to Greece in 1908.

Six years later the *A. G. Ropes* was built, of 2461 tons. One of that great fleet of wooden sailing ships built on the Eastern Seaboard of the United States which have come to be known as the 'Down-Easters', she is generally held to have been one of the finest of them. Named for the senior partner in her builders, I. F. Chapman, she became a barge in 1907. Opposite she is at sea, making a passage, and displaying several leads of rigging unfamiliar to those who knew only the later steel ships.

52. *A. G. ROPES on passage.*

53. *French barque NORMANDY, 732 tons gross, built at Honfleur in 1885 and owned by H. Auger ainé of Havre.*

54. RANGITAKI entering Port Chalmers.

Originally named *Scimitar*, this vessel soon came under the house-flag of the New Zealand Shipping Company to be the *Rangitiki*. Due to a mistake, the Maori name was mis-spelt as *Rangitaki*, and she had been so registered at Lloyds before the error was detected! Later she became the Norwegian *Dalston* and was ultimately hulked.

The New Zealand clippers made some very smart passages, and opposite is the *Auckland*, one of six splendid sisters of 1250 tons built for Patrick Henderson by Duncan's and run by Shaw Savill's till the beginning of this century. The others were: *Dunedin*, *Canterbury*, *Invercargill*, *Nelson* and *Wellington*. The *Auckland* passed to S. O. Stray of Haugesund in 1909, but disappeared soon afterwards.

The *Cairnbulg* was one of the pre-eminent wool clippers on the Australian run, being built at Aberdeen in 1874 and of 1567 tons. Here she is cut down to a barque, with her mizzen topgallantmast still fidded. Sold first to the Russians as the *Hellas*, she was bought by Denmark as the *Alexandra*, but posted missing on voyage from Newcastle N.S.W. to Panama. Later, one of her boats was picked up off the S. American coast, under the mate, and it seemed that she was abandoned in good order, simply because her provisions had run out! Later, the barque was found ashore on Albermarle Island with a broken back.

46

55. *AUCKLAND at Wellington.*

56. *CAIRNBULG off Gravesend.*

A 1000-ton full-rigged ship, the *Himalaya* was built by Pile of Sunderland in 1863. Shaw Savill's bought her in 1865 and she made 24 round voyages with cargo and passengers to New Zealand, some of which were not without incident. In 1880 she was converted to a barque, though the loss of the mizzen yards seldom detracted from, and often actually improved, a vessel's performance. Full-riggers had been *de rigueur* for years and both owners and masters were loath to admit that the mizzen yards tended to make a ship gripe on a wind and to throw her about with a following one. Ships were converted to barques, generally, as an economic measure though it is a moot point whether they might not have better so rigged from the outset! In 1899 the ship was sold to J. J. Moore of San Francisco and, two years later, she joined the fleet of the Alaska Packers of that port in the salmon cannery, being re-named *Star of Peru*. When they finally laid up their fleet she, being one of the smallest, was amongst the first to be sold, and became the hulk *Bourgainville* at Noumea.

Also built by Pile, in 1863, the *Laira* was only 492 tons and a trim little barque with her main skysail. First running for Shaw Savill, then for R. Stone of Auckland, and then for the N.Z.S. Co. She was owned by a Capt. Paterson in 1898 when lying at the Victoria wharf in Dunedin ready to sail for London with 1100 bales of wool. The Union s.s. *Wakatipu* refused to answer her helm and cut down the barque, which settled in six minutes (see Plate 58). Later, she was raised and put into the inter-colonial trade.

Another Pile-built ship was the *Sam Mendel* of 1861, 1034 tons, which was considered amongst the most beautiful iron ships. Her long bow had a phenomenally clean entrance and, with her square rig and raking masts, she made some fine passages, notably 68 days to Port Chalmers from London in 1876. In 1881, when racing one of Smith's 'Cities' and trying to improve her previous passage, she was partially dismasted in heavy weather and arrived as shown in Plate 59. About 1901 she became the Swedish *Charlonus* and, later, the *Hannah*, being broken up at Genoa in 1909. Her first owners were J. Coupland of Liverpool, and she was considered to have the lines of a yacht rather than of a merchant ship, yet she was hauling manganese ore whilst still under the Red Ensign.

48

57. *HIMALAYA as a barque in Wellington.*

58. *LAIRA cut down in Dunedin.*

59. SAM MENDEL in Port Chalmers, partially dismasted.

Built in 1876 for Anderson & Anderson, the *Harbinger* was a very lofty ship of 1506 tons with a gunter jibboom outside her normal one. She was said to be the only iron ship fitted with outside channels* and was certainly the last to be built to carry passengers. She carried 30 and was beautifully equipped. In 1890 she became one of Devitt & Moore's famous cadet ships for seven years, when she was sold to the Russians. The picture of her saloon came from the late D. R. Bolt, whose father was master of the ship.

Known as the last Blackwall frigate, the *Melbourne* was the last deepwater ship built at R. & H. Green's Blackwall yard for their line to Australia. Times had changed. Although she had the lines of the Blackwall frigates, she lacked the stern windows aft. In 1897 she replaced the *Harbinger* as a Devitt & Moore cadet ship and became the *Macquarrie*. Seven years later she was owned by J. Bryde of Sandefjord as the *Fortuna*, by then being barque rigged but, in 1909, was hulked in Sydney.

* The PORT JACKSON, a 4-masted barque built of iron in 1882, was fitted with outside channels.

50

60.   *The saloon in the HARBINGER.*

61.   *MACQUARRIE pitching into a sea. (Note the after boats griped outboard to provide more room on the poop for her passengers.)*

62. Trinidad cutter.

Time was when the only method of sea-travel was under sail and, when the early passenger steamers appeared (which carried quite a lot of sail, anyway), the sailing ship was still preferable. Latterly, apart from a few who made a passage simply for the experience of sail, passenger travel has been succeeded by the paddle steamer on short seas and the steamer—until the arrival of the flying machine. One of the last sailing types in the Western world to carry passengers were the West Indian cutters. This one, sailing across to Port o' Spain from San Fernando in a fresh trade, is making a good clip, the cargo and passengers all rather mixed up but, as she passed, clearly one of the most cheerful parties imaginable, and infinitely preferable to any motor-bus!

The fast West Indian schooners, which took their lineage from the Gloucester and Nova Scotian Grand Bank fishing schooners, also carried passengers occasionally. This one is off Port o' Spain.

52

63. *West Indian schooner off Port o' Spain.*

64. *Grand Banks schooner.*

The apprentice system, so prevalent in British deep-sea sailing ships, was certainly open to abuse, and it was thanks to the inspiration of Lord Brassey, coupled with the co-operation of Mr. T. Devitt, that Devitt & Moore started their great sail-training scheme in which cadets were carried in a more enlightened fashion in vessels which were paying their way as merchantmen. No other company could match them for both standards and continuity of ships and service.

One of their best known masters was Capt. F. W. Corner, who was mate in the *Rodney* and *Hesperus*, and then master in the *Harbinger* (in which vessel the eminent sea-writer Frank Bullen was second mate), and subsequently in the *Macquarrie*. He left her in 1903 to take command of the Federal 4-masted steamer *Norfolk*. This ship was built in an age when steamers had ceased to carry any sail and, in 1906, when in the South Indian Ocean, she lost her propellor. Oddly, perhaps, only one other man in the vessel besides Capt. Corner had been in sail, but he managed to jury-rig her with derricks and tarpaulins and to sail her the 1400-odd miles to Fremantle in 11 days.

The s.s. *Carlisle*, in similar circumstances, was sailed from some 300 miles south-east of Yokohama 3200 miles to the Philippines in 86 days under an incredible rig in which all the sails, including their twine, was derived from rice bags! Both events were as sterling performances as they were exceptional, and could never occur in modern super-tankers or container vessels! Nevertheless, it cannot be gainsaid that in recent years there have been emergencies, including the abandonment of vessels, in which sail-trained men would clearly have been of great benefit. Contrary to the modern belief that a man can be 'sail-trained' during a short course in an over-manned ship, it takes time. The skills of sticks and string have little place in an electronic age with neo-robot ships, but their influences on character are by no means to be despised.

Most efforts in this direction fail due to the necessity of carrying too many boys or cadets in a vessel nowadays, in order to make her economically viable, and the answer may lie in some of those craft whose form has not changed materially in centuries. Square-rig and high-masting do not lend themselves to short courses, which demand low freeboard and specific duties for each boy.

65. s.s. *NORFOLK*, *disabled and jury-rigged.*

66. *Proa regatta.*

In the context of the preceding comment it might be worth considering the Flying Proas. The various types of proa (or prau) are legion and it is not intended to confuse the issue in this picture book by expanding on the theme. Hailing from the Celebes, these craft were termed 'flying' proas due to their great speed. Whether amongst Thames bargemen: Gloucester schooner-men, Brixham trawlers, or elsewhere, there is always an urge for an annual regatta. Most of these pictures were taken on such an occasion. Note in Plate 68 the minimal beam of the actual hull: the outrigger and the balance taking the weight of sail and spar. Then observe the vast area of the single sail and the very expertise involved in handling the craft at speed, each man virtually balanced on a bamboo strut of the outrigger. Yachtsmen, have they the courage, have much to learn from these craft which provide a sensation of pure sailing *par excellence*, whilst the fact that each man has his own clear responsibility might appeal to those involved on character training schemes. Proas are cheap to build!

67. *Proa.*

69.

68.

70.   *Celebes Proas.*

57

71. *Proas, racing.*

72. *Flying Proas.* 58

73. *Proa.*

74. *Kapal off Macassar.*   59

75. Philippine dug-out proa.

Whereas the Flying proas were used, in former times, for acts of piracy when occasion demanded, the term *'proa'* can include almost any undecked native craft from Malaysia to the Philippines, and some may even have platforms. They may be dug-out or plank built. Plate 75 shows a very primitive dug-out *prau* in the Philippines with a spritsail—the sprit consisting of a thick bamboo. The different varieties of this craft have many different names dependent on their location, their form of hull and the trade or purpose for which they are built. Those which are permanently decked are termed *'kapal'*. There are, however, numerous other types of open craft which are *not* within the generic term *prau* or *prao*, such as the Malay *payang*, and many others. Plate 74 shows a *kapal* off Macassar. The study of these craft, together with the various canoes and other types of the area, is an involved one, since different areas have minor differences with different names.

60

76. Paduakan.

Also termed a *pediwak*, with a hull normally of teak or giam wood, the hollow, sharp bow is lower than the main hull. With a curved, raking stem, the transom stern has a tall superstructure supported by cross timbers. The tripod mast well may find its origin in ancient Babylon, each foot being bolted into a socket so that the whole assemblage can be lowered. Formerly rigged with lugsails, gaffs became common and the lowers brailed to the mast. The bowsprit is stepped in the forward bulkhead and supported each side by two planks, while the steering depends upon two, narrow quarter rudders which can be raised when not in use. Sometimes voyaging to Singapore, varying in length from 32 to 90 feet, they pitch heavily and make a lot of leeway due to the high poop. Modern versions had wire standing rigging set up with dead-eyes and lanyards, and cables of 2 in. palm fibre—a strange mixture of old and new. The *paduakan* should not be confused with the *prao julung-julung* or Malay *Penjaleng*.

61

77. In the London Graving Dock.

All the major ports were a mass of masts and yards in the days of sail. London River saw as great a variety as almost any, being not only the port for a major capital but a great *entrepôt* port for the continent. In the Graving dock (above) the skysail-yard full-rigger alongside the 4-masted barque is a real beauty. Surrey Docks are now all filled in, with Lavender and Acorn Ponds and all the rest of that complex with its sweet scent of discharged timber. The square-riggers and all the small craft—the barges, schooners, brigs and so forth about their business are vanished now. Few of the ships are remembered or recorded in the histories. It was always the first flight which stole the thunder. Who knows the *Beemah*, in the centre of Plate 80? An iron barque of 954 tons, she was owned by Herron & Hellon of Liverpool, who bought her from T. H. Johnson of the same port. She was built by Wm. Hamilton in 1876.

When the Thames froze in 1895 the channel and traffic was much reduced. Gravesend Reach was one of the busiest and most fascinating stretches of water in the world for its multiplicity of craft.

62

78.   *Gravesend Reach frozen, looking towards Tilbury where square-riggers can be seen in the dock.*

79. Surrey Commercial Dock. (Note that one barque has her jibboom topped up.)

80. S.W. India Dock, London. (Barque BEEMAH centre, bows on.)

81. *Gravesend Reach frozen in 1895. Looking downstream with a brigantine, a topgallant- and a topsail-schooner under way, and numerous sailing craft at Lobster buoys.*

82. The VIRGO's figurehead.

That so many ships changed their names so often created a clear cause of confusion, though this occurred more often with the big deepwatermen than with the short-sea traders and smaller craft. Anyone walking round a dock and seeing this figurehead on a barque named *Virgo* might have had occasion to pause and wonder, but the iron barque in question had been built in Glasgow in 1869 as the *Endymion*: a name which she retained under subsequent Norwegian ownership from 1900 to 1914, and she only became the *Virgo* when sold to Sweden in that latter year. Whether the likeness is such that Selene, Goddess of the Moon, would have become so enamoured of its subject is, perhaps open to question.

Of 759 tons, the vessel is sometimes confused with another Swedish *Virgo*, which was sold by Mathias Hansen of Kristianssand after he had had her for 20 years under her original British name of *Closeburn*. She was also an iron barque, of 886 tons. It was sometimes possible to see four or five vessels with the same name in one day.

66

83. VIRGO, ex ENDYMION.

84. FRANCESCO GUISEPPE I.

Ships of all nations visited London River. Here the *Guiseppe Francesco I* flies the Italian ensign above the pilot flag (H), with a small stumpy barge, her mizzen sheeted to the rudder, under her stern. Originally one of the 'Falls' Line of Glasgow—the nine 4-masters built by Russell's of which the first six were all full-rigged—she was the *Falls of Afton* when built in 1882. A very strong ship and fast off the wind, her passages proved to be variable. She was 1810 tons nett and sold to the Italians, being registered in the Austro-Hungarian port of Lussngrunde and owned by F. G. Leve. Alex Bech of Tvedestrand bought her in 1907 and, oddly perhaps, restored her original name. She was sunk by a U-boat in the Channel in 1917 when owned in Christiania. Her sister ship, the *Falls of Dee*, suffered the same fate in the same year, being then the *Teie* owned by a Tonsberg whaling firm and bound home with whale oil.

85.   *TRANSOCEAN, s.s. MINNESOTA (Atlantic Transport Line) and a schooner.*

London was one of the last ports where square-riggers might be seen with any regularity. The *Transocean* was built of steel at Grimstad in 1891. (The Norwegians did not only build in wood!) Of 737 tons, she was first owned by Peder Olsen of Arendal who sold her in 1897 to Chr. Klöcker of the same port. Th. Bentzen bought her in 1906 and, in all this time, she was named *Robert Scrafton*, but became the *Transocean* in 1922 when sold to Malmö in Sweden. H. Daniel owned her in 1924 but she passed to Finland in 1926 when this picture was taken and when painted ports were becoming uncommon. Her fore royal yard is either on deck or no longer carried, and it will be seen that her main royal is still clewed up to the quarters. By this time barques of her size were scarcely economic, and she was sold to Havana interests to be a hulk for £2150 when lying in the Thames. There were not many trades left open to her.

69

86. ALASTOR, by the wind.

Last of the onker barques to trade to the Thames, and sporting a main skysail above royals when built in 1875 in Sunderland for Penney's of Shoreham, she was the only skysail-yarder owned in the port and, of 860 tons, was long running to New Zealand on charter to Shaw, Savill.

In 1905 she passed to the Stray family of Kristianssand and, in 1928, to the Consul Schröder of Hangö.

Those familiar with Arthur Briscoe's etchings will recognise this famous little barque in which he once made a passage and which was often one of his 'subjects'. Had he shown a man descending the lee rigging, he would doubtless have been much criticised, since it was not normal seamanlike practice. However, the camera cannot lie!

Caught in London in 1939, she was moored at Tollesbury and, after a sad period as a restaurant at Ramsgate, she was broken up.

70

88. *ALASTOR in Mariehamn Harbour—barque CARMEN beyond.*

87. *ALASTOR in Portsmouth, 1937.*

89.

90.   *Old-fashioned 'Armstrong's Patent' windlasses seen in the Thames.*

72

91. Built as a barque for the China trade in 1866, named CLETA and composite-built, she became the Swedish NELLY AND MATHILDE and finally the Finnish FRIDEBORG, running in the 'onker' trade until she was condemned in 1937 after stranding off Kalix.

92. Unlike lumber, the short off-cuts from the saw-mills carried by the 'onkers' made an awkward surface on which to work the ship when at sea.

93. *ABRAHAM RYDBERG towing down the Thames astern of the well-known sailing ship tug ARCADIA.*

Colours, deck-erections and even angles of view sometimes make ship recognition difficult. As the *Hawaiian Isles*, built in 1894 for M. Nelson of Honolulu, she was then rigged with skysails on main and mizzen. These became discarded and, after a period owned by Welch of San Francisco, she joined the Alaska Packers fleet as the *Star of Greenland* in 1914. When that fleet was laid up, in the 1920's, she was amongst them but, in 1928, was sold to the Abraham Rydberg Sail-training Association and, in 1929, loaded with barley, made the last homeward passage from 'Frisco round the Horn. She is leaving in Plate 94. She was then altered, being given a midship section and cadet accommodation and traded to and from Australia, mainly to London, until 1939. The last 4-masted barque with single topgallants, she also set triangular courses (Pl. 96) and a jib-headed pole spanker with no gaff. It was, perhaps, strange that triangular courses should have been so favoured by cadet ships latterly when they, alone, had large enough crews to handle the sheets and tacks quickly and efficiently. Altering her schedules during Hitler's war, she finally passed to the Portuguese and became a full-powered motor-ship named the *Foz de Douro* when, although her mizzen mast remained intact, together with the other three lower masts, she ceased to be a sailing ship. In the grain trade, from Australia, she invariably came home via the Cape route.

74

95. *ABRAHAM RYDBERG in Millwall Dock.*

94. *ABRAHAM RYDBERG leaving San Francisco.*

96. *ABRAHAM RYDBERG in the Channel.*

97. *The DISCOVERY in Antarctic Seas on her first voyage with Captain Scott.*

98. *Apparently discharging a cargo of matting, the Dutch barque MARTINA JOHANNA lies in a London Dock. Built by J. K. Smit at Krimpen in 1891 of 1408 tons gross, and owned by P. van der Hoog of that port.*

99. The famous HAUGHTY BELLE—built like a yacht with a counter stern.

Great indeed have been the changes in the shipping using London River over the last forty years. In 1934 it was possible to write of the sailing barges: "It is hard to find a picture of the Thames without one or more of these beautiful vessels lending a touch of grace and colour to the scene. One cannot even think of the lower river without the barges, some under way, with their reddish brown canvas full and drawing and carrying them smoothly about their business, while others lie at anchor with sails brailed up waiting for the tide that sluices past their sides to turn in their favour". Today not one is left carrying cargo under sail. All that now remain are the few maintained by enthusiasts as yacht-barges or for prestige purposes, with those like the *Thalatta* and the *Sir Alan Herbert* of the East Coast Sail Trust which give adventure training to children of school age, and the *Pudge* and the *Centaur* of the Thames Barge Sailing club.

100.   Racing spritsail barges— *HAUGHTY BELLE* (*with white hull*) *and CLARA.*

101. BLACK DUCK, after shooting bridges at Rochester under sail.

Yet it was not their beauty, so dramatically emphasised in the pictures of the *Clara* and *Haughty Belle* racing (Plates 99 and 100) that ensured their survival for so long. This was wholly due to the superb efficiency of their spritsail rig, with the huge mainsail that could be brailed up with a winch like a theatre curtain, and the 'go-anywhere' versatility of their shallow flat-bottom hulls, with lee-boards that could be lowered to give lateral resistance on which they could spin round like a racing dinghy. Fantastically handy under sail, they could work their way up the shallowest creek to load, and then safely transport their cargoes coast-wise or cross-seas, winter and summer alike, anywhere within the Home Trade limits, from Ushant to the Elbe. Nor were bridges any obstacle to their progress, for masts and sails were so rigged that all could be lowered down on deck by easing away on a single rope, the stay-fall tackle. After passing

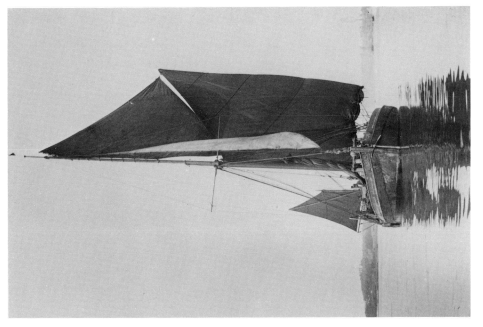

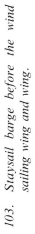

103. *Staysail barge before the wind sailing wing and wing.*

102. *One of A. Hutson's 'spreeties'. The sprit was always to starboard.*

104. Barges without topmasts, like the CLYDE of 1883, were termed 'Stumpies'.

under the bridge, the stay-fall was taken to the windlass, and everything was wound up again, as is being done aboard the *Black Duck* of London, Plate 101, photographed after she had shot the Rochester bridges under sail in 1929. This routine was taken as a matter of course, and the bargemen thought nothing of it.

106. *THURSDAY of Rochester. (One of the Blue Circle Fleet.)*

105. *Shrubsall's coasting barge VICUNIA with bowsprit and racing flag.*

107.   HIBERNIA of Rochester, 45 tons, built at Strood in 1899.

It seems almost incredible that so large a craft could be sailed by a crew of only two all told, yet such was the normal complement of a barge able to carry up to 180 tons of cargo. Only the biggest, like the

108. Coasting barge, her topmast gone, ashore at Kingsdown.

four 300-ton Everards, carried a third hand. This was because the sails, which in a Coasting Class barge would have a total area in excess of 6000 square feet, could all be both set and stowed without

85

leaving the deck. Only to pass the gaskets when making a snug stow of the topsail was it necessary to go aloft. Easy manoeuvring was ensured by sheeting the small mizzen to the end of the rudder* so that, as the helm was put down when tacking, the sail was pulled up to windward, acting like a rudder in the air, and, with the foresail held aback by a bowline secured to the forward shroud, there was a turning couple pushing the bows one way and the stern the other until the sails had filled on the new tack. Reefing was quickly effected by partially brailing up the mainsail and, in narrow waters, the barge could be handled perfectly under her topsail, foresail and mizzen alone, as may be seen in Plate 109 where the *J.W.N.* is moving up slowly to moor off Gravesend with only the topsail left set.

Yet, for all their bluff bows and flat-bottomed hulls, the sailing barges were far from slow. In the Thames Race of 1928, for instance, sailed in half a gale of wind, the *Vigilant*, winner of the Coasting Class, averaged twelve knots through the water on the run down to the Mouse, and crossed the finishing line at Gravesend, after beating back over a spring ebb tide, before the vessels at anchor there had swung to the young flood, sailing fifty-six miles, half of them dead to windward against the tide, in just over six hours.

Barge racing in the Thames began in 1863, and continued annually, with a few interruptions caused by wars and other troubles, until the Centenary Race in 1963, which was the last for working barges. Since then, the traditions have been carried on by privately owned craft, and there is no finer sight in the Estuaries today than a keenly fought contest between racing barges in a good breeze. Long may these survive, but the costs are rising astronomically. In 1926, a hand-sewn flax barge's mainsail could be made for £47-10s, and would last from seven to twelve years. Today, fifty years later, a suit of sails for a barge will leave no change out of £2500. It is hardly surprising, therefore, that, commercially, the trading barges have reached the end of the road. With their passing disappeared a watermanship *par excellence*, often the bane of pilots in big ships on this once crowded river who might suddenly encounter a dozen or more barges close-tacking in a narrow reach through which they had to find a way.

*See Pl. 84.

86

110. *Smeed Dean's MYRTLE loading bricks. Built 1880 at Milton, Kent.*

109. *J.W.N. reducing sail before anchoring.*

111. Barges, many with Smeed Dean's 'bobs', waiting for freights.

112. Racing barges, 1932. REMINDER leading PHOENICIAN.

114. *GERTRUDE MAY'S mate using setting boom in narrow waters.*

113. *Kent and Essex farmers sent their hay by sea in barges called 'Stackies' to feed London's horses.*

115. *The flatiron collier WANDLE upsets the 1935 barge race trying to save her tide.*

116. *REDOUBTABLE, SARA, and REMINDER in the 47th Thames match, June 26th, 1932.*

117. Declining years in Anchor Bay, Gravesend, once the home of many bawleys.

For as long as London has been a city, fish has formed a staple diet for the population, and craft of many kinds have been evolved to cater for this need, from the small double-ended clinker-built Peter Boat, which has endured until recent years as the Medway doble, to the big Barking well smacks which migrated to Yarmouth in the mid-nineteenth century. Among the last to survive were the Leigh bawleys, of which an excellent example was the *Ethel*, Plate 118, photographed in 1910 by the late Mr. J. P. Hodge. These were employed both in shrimping and in that form of fishing known as stow-boating. They set an enormous spread of canvas for their size, being about 35 feet overall. Today sails have been replaced by the ubiquitous marine engine but, in Plate 117, a solitary derelict smack keeps company in retirement with an old bawley.

91

118.   Leigh bawley ETHEL trawling under sail, October 1910.

119. *Whitstable Oyster dredgers are racing here with mainsails reefed.*

120. Manoeuvring before the start of the Whitstable Oyster dredgers race.

The fame of Whitstable oysters has extended over two millennia, even to the extent of being sent to Rome during the occupation! Oyster smacks might be found in the Essex rivers about Colchester, at Mylor, near Falmouth, and elsewhere, with local differences in rig and form. Those around Whitstable and Herne Bay, (usually bearing the 'F' registration for Faversham) were about 35-45 feet in length as a rule, and were not entirely to a standard type, since some had jib-headed topsails and some jack-yards, and there were other, minor differences. At the turn of the century, the fleet numbered about 80.

Although patently cutter-rigged, they were always known locally as 'yawls' (which they never were), and it is this sort of local terminology which often causes confusion in the usage of nautical terms.

Like most local craft the world over, there was an annual regatta and, in Plate 119 the topsails are not only fast, but each craft has a single reef in the mainsail. There was, of course, a point of contact between such local craft and the big ships in the Estuary, although the former were seldom to be found in the main channels.

94

121.   The DISCOVERY leaving Cape Town, bound south.

In this age of ship preservation, it is a crying scandal that one of Britain's most historic vessels, the *Discovery*, should lie in the heart of London bereft of her yards. Although similar to a whaler, she was built by Alex. Stephens (who launched so many of the steam whalers) for Antarctic research. Her career in this respect is well-known. Of 736 tons and 179.9 feet in length, her name is indissolubly linked with Capt. Scott, being owned by the Hudson's Bay Company. By 1929 she was being used by the Falkland Islands Dependencies for whale research work and was then laid up in the East India Dock, fully rigged. Now she is moored on the Thames Embankment, but her yards had been 'lost' during the war and even now, after thirty years, they have never been replaced. This disgraceful fact may seem to be incredible since there are numerous societies dedicated to the preservation of historic ships. Originally with single topgallants, she was later given double topgallant yards (Pl. 121 and 122). Her rudder, slung on one pintle, could easily be unshipped, as could her screw. A sluggish sailer, her masts were stepped too far aft.

95

122. The DISCOVERY becalmed off Cape Town.

123. The TERRA NOVA, built in 1884 by Alex. Stephen, spent years whaling and sealing in Greenland waters. When this picture was taken she had been chartered by the British government to go to the relief of the DISCOVERY.

124. The auxiliary whaler HOPE at Aberdeen in 1873, when new.

Of 452 tons, the *Hope* was the last of the Peterhead whalers to be built. Whilst the screw and funnel might properly preclude such vessels from a book about sailing ships, they did use their sail a good deal, and never used the engines when actually whale hunting, due to the whales' acute hearing. Twice she lost her screw in the ice. As originally designed she was to have single topsails, but in fact was rigged with double yards. The whalers were always distinctive by the number of boats carried, and it will be noted that she not only has a bentinck boom, but that, like many of the whalers, she has a short upper gaff and a brailing gaff topsail. Sold to Dundee in 1891, she was wrecked on Byron Island in the Gulf of St. Lawrence in 1901 with 5000 seals aboard. When he was a medical student, Sir Arthur Conan Doyle made a voyage to the Greenland Seas in her as medical officer. She might have made a good setting for one of his novels!

125. FERREIRA, ex CUTTY SARK, arriving at Cape Town, dismasted.

The fame of the *Cutty Sark* is too great to be recounted here. She was undoubtedly one of the most successful clippers ever built, if not *the* most successful, though this might be open to debate. That she survived her peers certainly enhanced her reputation. She had passed to the Portuguese and, under their flag, was towed into Cape Town dismasted in 1916. When re-rigged, as in Plate 127, she was a barquentine instead of a full-rigged ship. This is something for which the Portuguese have sometimes been blamed, but they had little option, since it was just not possible to re-rig the ship in her original form in Cape Town at that time. They had bought a number of fine clippers, and were always fine seamen. Later, her appearance was changed when they gave her painted ports, which did not suit her. Thus she is painted in Falmouth Harbour just after Capt. W. H. Dowman, formerly master of the full-rigger *Dovenby*, had bought her back to the British flag and before he had her re-rigged. Now, of course, she is preserved in a dry-dock at Greenwich, perfect aloft.

126. *FERREIRA in Carrick Roads (Falmouth). FOUDROYANT beyond.*

127. *FERREIRA in Cape Town, re-rigged as a barquentine.*

99

128. SELENE dismasted, in Cape Town.

Cape Town was a great square-rigger port and, in virtue of its position, many lame ducks put in there for repairs. Such a one was the Norwegian barque *Selene*, built in Rostock in 1889 for H. F. Ulrichs of Bremen. She took a real battering when her top-hamper came down on top of her, and it is always incredible that there was not more injury on such occasions.

The *Hawaii* was built by McMillan's of Dumbarton for Hind Rolph in 1900 and was of 1085 tons gross. Here she is arriving in Table Bay with a deck-load of lumber. Later she was cut down to a bald-headed schooner as the *Ethel M. Sterling*, and was finally the Mexican *Hidalgo*.

Slightly bigger, of 1385 tons gross, the *Alta* was built in the same year for San Francisco owners but was later, as here, registered in Manila. She, too, is arriving in Cape Town with lumber.

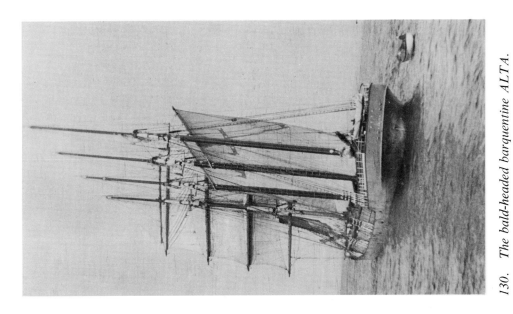

130.   *The bald-headed barquentine ALTA.*

129.   *HAWAII arriving in Table Bay.*

131. LAHAINA lying in Cape Town.

Also owned by Hind, Rolph of San Francisco, and much the same size as the *Hawaii*, the *Lahaina* was built of wood in Oakland and smacks of her country of origin with her fore skysail. In these three barquentines we see three different forms of foremast rigging. The *Woodburn* was not a barque with much aesthetic appeal, being bald-headed and built for capacity for Shankland's 'Burn' line in 1896, being their second ship of the name. She was sold to Finland in 1909 and, ten years later, became Capt. Erikson's eleventh acquisition, being finally hulked in Suva in 1926.

The fidded mizzen topgallant-mast of the *Glenshee* denotes that she was full-rigged when built in 1882. Here she takes in her fore upper topsail as she enters Table Bay. This vessel once survived a really terrible pooping and, finally, grounded outside Arendal with a coal cargo but was salved, only to be towed to Copenhagen ship-breakers, arriving half-full of water. She had had a long and useful life.

102

132.   *WOODBURN in Cape Town.*

133.   *GLENSHEE reducing sail in Table Bay.*

103

134. Cape Town Docks, circa 1898.

A light ship tends to look heavy, but the two pictures opposite demonstrate how an angle of view, coupled with the paint and the actual rig of a ship, can mislead the eye. Both are Norwegian 4-masted barques. The *Audun* was originally the British *Armadale*, of 2015 tons, built of iron by A. Stephen for Roxburgh's. She has single topgallant yards and her painted ports, painted up from the black stripe, are above a light grey paint.

The *Valerie* was built in the same year as the *Clan Buchanan*, and was Thos. Dunlop's first four-master. Not so fast as the full-riggers which preceded her, she was nevertheless a most successful vessel, running mainly to the West Coast of North America, Australia and, to a lesser extent, to Japan. In 1909 she passed to Tomas Berg of Stavanger, to be renamed *Valerie*. The Norwegians had a good eye for a ship and it should not pass unnoticed how many of their purchases were built of iron, as distinct from steel. When owned by P. Larsen of Liknesund, she was torpedoed in April 1917.

Admittedly the *Valerie* was 2072 tons, but she was actually two feet shorter. The effect of the two photographs seen in juxtaposition is to make her seem a very much bigger ship.

104

135.   *AUDUN, ex ARMADALE, in Cape Town.*

136.   *VALERIE, ex CLAN BUCHANAN, in Cape Town.*

105

137. TWEEDSDALE.

The interest attaching to the *Tweedsdale* lies in the fact that she was the first conventional 4-masted barque to be built—in 1875. Being 1403 tons and 244.4 feet in length, she was also one of the smallest. The motive was to lighten the ship aloft, since the initial building of heavily rigged full-riggers had led to a spate of dismastings. Her career was not exceptional and, after Scandinavian ownership as the *Rolf* and *Germot*, she was hulked in Lisbon in 1922.

The first American essay into this rig was the huge *Shenandoah* of 3154 tons and almost 300 feet in length, with trucks 217 feet above the deck. Famous for her performances and handling, it is said, like a 'knockabout schooner', she could load 5300 tons. She was built by and for Sewall's of Bath, Maine, who afterwards built the only steel American 4-masters, and, under her famous master, Jim Murphy, with her three skysails, became one of the most famous ships afloat. In 1910 she was cut down to a towing barge. Her fame was such that per picture graced many official American shipping documents.

138. *SHENANDOAH.* (*Note the extent of her railings.*)

139. EDWARD SEWALL off Galveston, Texas.

Sewall of Bath, who had built the big wooden 4-masted barques like the *Shenandoah*, *Roanoke* and *Susquehanna*, was the only American builder to launch this rig in steel. There were only eight of them, and the *Edward Sewall*, built for the firm's own account and sister to the *Arthur Sewall* (though a little bigger) was one of the largest. Built in 1899 she measured 332 x 45.3 x 25.5 ft. and, at her best, could load over 5000 tons of cargo. In 1913-14, after twice putting back to Bahia with a snapped bowsprit, she spent 67 days—atrocious days—before she doubled the Horn, but she was on the whole a smart ship for her size, latterly being owned by the Alaska Packers Association of San Francisco as the *Star of Shetland* from 1922 until, after a period when their fleet was laid up, she was sold to Japanese shipbreakers in Osaka in 1936 and sailed over by a Japanese crew, only to arrive in tow almost totally dismasted. These ships were readily distinguishable by their unusual wheel-houses which, if unsightly, were extremely comfortable, containing more than the wheel.

140.   PONAPE—perfect sailing conditions, 1935.

141. BREIDABLIK.

Building so many wooden ships and buying so many fine iron and steel ones second-hand, it is easy to forget that the Norwegians purchased such vessels as the *Breidablik* on the stocks. Bruusgaard, Klosterud & Co. of Drammen bought her in 1891 and named her for the palace of the Norse sun-god, Baldur. Of 2416 tons, she was wrecked in Delagoa Bay in 1905.

The *Poltalloch* was built in Belfast by Workman & Clark for Potter's, of London, in 1893. In 1900 she ran ashore on Clatsop Sands at the mouth of the Columbia River to an extent that she was high and dry at low water. It was assumed that she would be engulfed like other ships, but her master, Capt. Young, ran out 300-fathom manila hawsers with a spring of some 30 feet and, as the seas shuddered the ship, they took in the slack, getting her back in deep water **after a year**—a unique occurrence. Latterly owned by Eschen & Miner, of Victoria, B.C. when her hull was painted a dull red, she was torpedoed in the First World War.

110

142.   POLTALLOCH as a new ship.   2254 tons gross.

143.   FORT GEORGE in graving dock at Port Chalmers.

Of an earlier vintage, the *Fort George* was built by Workman & Clark in Belfast for Clark & Service of Glasgow, being later owned in Limerick. This picture gives a good idea of her deck layout.

    The splendid looking *Strathgryfe* is seen with the hulk of a small sailing vessel and a paddle tug alongside. Built in 1890 by Russell's for MacGillivrays, of 2276 tons, she was re-named *Margretha* when sold to the Germans in 1910 and, in the short time that they had her, they improved her sailing performances dramatically, as they did with a number of their bought vessels. In the first war she was seized by Portugal and named *Graciosa*, but was sunk by a German submarine in 1918. The ship had a reputation for speed even when under the British flag and, although she succeeded the best looking 4-masters with masts of unequal height, she was nevertheless an impressive vessel with deep single topgallantsails though, by the time she was built, spike bowsprits had replaced jibbooms.

144.   *STRATHGRYFE loading in Port Chalmers.*

145. JEANNETTE FRANÇOISE.

Apart from a number built in France, all but some 18 of all 4-masted barques (excepting wooden ones) were built in Britain. One of the only two built in Holland was the *Jeannette Françoise* at Krimpen in 1893. Later she became the *Carl*, under Krabbenhoft & Bock of Hamburg who ran her to the West Coast of South America. After the war she passed as reparations to O. Kverndal of Tvedestrand as the *Souvenir*, but the slump killed her and she was broken up in 1925.

The *Eulomene* was Fernies' only 4-master, having been built as a full-rigger but later cut down to a barque, as seen in Plate 146. All the Fernie ships had the suffix '-omene'. The matter of any advantage (or the reverse) in being rigged as a ship has already been discussed (page 48) but it may also be observed that the advantages of such a battery of staysails is a matter of no less debate, since their drawing power was often outweighed by their effect on the square sails.

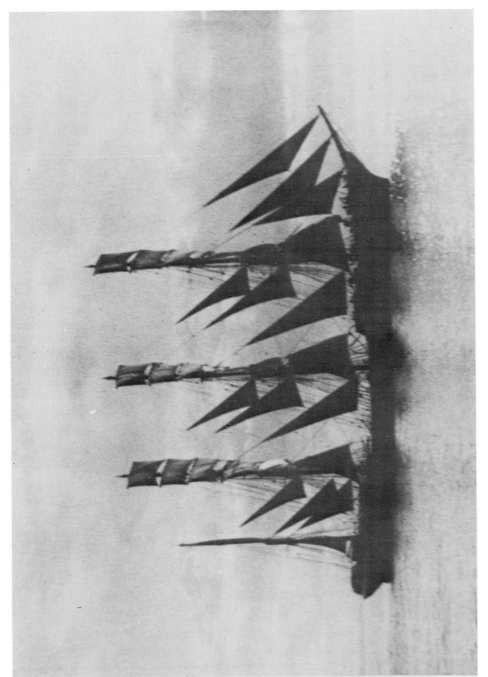

146.   *Fernie's EULOMENE.*

147.   ADOLPHE wrecked on the Oyster Bank, Newcastle, N.S.W.

One of the finest of the magnificent fleet of A. D. Bordes of Dunkirk, the *Adolphe* was built in 1902 by the Chantiers de France of that port. Of 3245 tons gross, she was entering Newcastle, N.S.W. two years later with a cargo of cement from Antwerp astern of the 849 barque *Regent Murray* with two tugs ahead. The *Regent Murray* had one tug, the *Newburgh*, which parted her line and she drove ashore on to the Oyster Bank. Almost immediately the *Victoria*, one of the *Adolphe*'s tugs, parted her line and the other—the *Hero*—could not hold her and she went ashore just astern of the barque, never to come off. The photograph was taken from the *Regent Murray* minutes after the strandings, and sprays can already be seen reaching as high as the *Adolphe*'s topsail yards. Shortly afterwards, she was in sorry state, and soon a wreck.

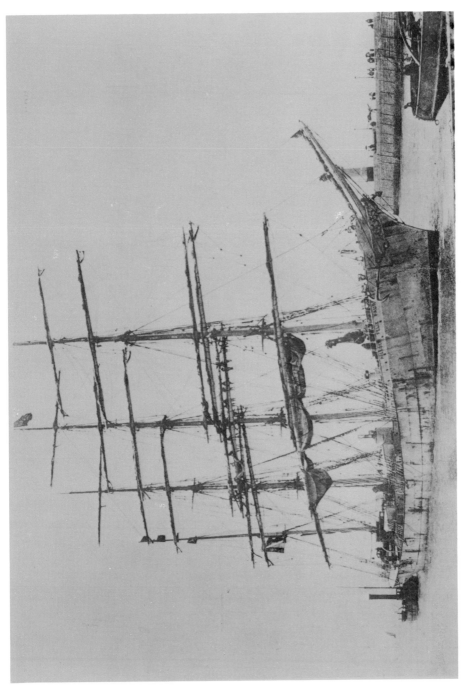

148. *PRESIDENT FELIX FAURÉ. Built for Courblet and Brown in 1896, the latter had been master in American ships and it was probably his influence which gave this vessel skysails, which were unusual in French-built vessels. She was wrecked on the Antipodes Islands in 1908, loaded with nickel ore.*

149. *4-master VALPARAISO lying off Caleta Coloso, October 1924.*

The ships of A. D. Bordes were just as smart and efficient as those of the more famous Hamburg 'P' fleet, and generally engaged in the same trade. Here the *Valparaiso* is loading her last cargo, riding to two anchors under the shadow of the Andes, before being broken up in 1926. Built in 1902, she was sister to the *Antonin*, sunk by the *See-Adler*. (See page 292.)

A Russian 4-masted barque in trade was a rare sight after the revolution and after Finland had become independent. The *Tovarisch* was originally the *Lauriston*, a British 4-masted full-rigger of 3500 tons deadweight built for the Calcutta jute trade, but was reduced to a barque before her owners, Galbraith and Moorehead, sold her to Duncan's Empire line in 1905. After a fresh change of owners she went to Russia and these pictures were taken in the Solent when she was engaged in a sort of comic opera voyage, of which the details are too long to be described here, but which are summarised in *Square-Riggers—The Final Epoch, 1921-1958.*

150.   TOVARISCH making sail, 1927.

151.   TOVARISCH loosing sail, 1927.

119

152. A barque and a schooner.

The barque above has not been identified, but certain of her features lead to the belief that she was built on the eastern seaboard of America. Sidelights were not commonly carried at sea until well on into the 1880's, except perhaps under the land or in more congested waters. American vessels, in particular, were prone to seize their side-light brackets onto their mizzen rigging, as in this case. When one considers how the courses projected beyond the sides of a vessel, it is clear that their utility was of dubious value to any ship fairly fine on either bow!

The two sister ships opposite were typical examples of French Bounty building with their ample poops and foc's'le heads. Built for Corblet's nickel ore trade, they passed successively to the Cie. Navale de l'Oceanie of Havre as *Sainte Catherine* and *Sainte Marguerite* and later to A. D. Bordes as *Seine* and *Blanche*. The *Blanche* was sunk by a U-boat after a $2\frac{1}{2}$-hour gun battle in 1917. The *Seine* was scuttled in Havre with her cotton cargo afire in 1919 but raised, and scrapped during the slump in 1923.

153. ERNEST SIEGFRIED, later SAINTE CATHERINE, later BLANCHE.

154. EMILIE SIEGFRIED, later SAINTE MARGUERITE, later SEINE.

155. *After wheel-box removed—*
PAMIR.

156. *Wheel-box removed—*
OMEGA, ex DRUMCLIFF.

In smaller and older sailing ships, the wheel was simply at the end of a barrel with a rope wound round it and led through leading blocks on the sides of the deck and back to the tiller head. Thus, as the wheel was turned, the tiller turned to one side or the other.

As ships became bigger, screw gear was used. Plate 155 shows the principle. The *Pamir* happens to have a double wheel, but its shaft had a screw—half being left-handed and half right-handed. Thus, as the wheel (and shaft) are turned, the sleeves on either side, working on guide rods, are moved in opposite directions and these in turn move the connecting rods to the crosshead which operates the rudder head. This crosshead is immediately abaft the wheel.

122

157. *PAMIR—wheel, crosshead and connecting rod.*

158. *OMEGA's steering apparatus.*

159. *In Callao with the Peruvian barque MAIPO beyond, the OMEGA has her wheel-box removed to display screw shaft, sleeves, connecting rods and crosshead.*

160.   NIVELLE as a new ship.

J. Hardie's were the last British company to own 4-masted barques. (The *Garthpool* is excluded, being registered in Montreal.) The *Nivelle* was built in 1897 but, in 1906, was wrecked near Antofagasta.

The *Vimiera*, sister to the *Pyrenees* which became famous for being beached afire on Manga Reva Island (which gave her her subsequent name) and to Clink's *Thistle* and *Valkyrie*, was built in 1891. Slightly smaller than the *Nivelle*, she still has single top-gallants. Here she has the wind aft: mainsail hauled up: main canvas pulling aback and all fore-and-aft sails in. For some reason, few ship-masters would tack to leeward—sailing a little off the wind with all sails full. The extra speed more than compensated for the extra mileage, and made for better steering too, in bad weather. Change was generally anathema to these conservative gentlemen!

124

161. *VIMIERA.*

162. *ARCHIBALD RUSSELL was Hardie's last survivor. Here, owned by Capt.
Gustaf Erikson, she is loading timber at Sundsvall in 1925. Unfortunately, she
became frozen in for the winter!*

163. Fire-wood cutter in Stockholm.

Many of the last Scandinavian square-rigger crews received their sea-baptism in either the small, cutter-rigged jakt* or in the 2-masted galleass.† The former had a standing gaff with a brailing mainsail, a topsail and three headsails. Built in the Åland Islands or Roslagen, the northern part of the Stockholm archipelago, often on a frozen bay in winter, launching was no problem in the spring! Generally, they carried firewood or sand for the cement factories.

In the remainder of Sweden was built the galleass, which might be said to be an enlarged version of the jakt, with two masts and, in some sense, to be the Baltic counterpart of the Thames sailing barge. The brailing lowers rendered them easy for two men to handle and, as can be seen, they often carried large deck cargoes. The vessel shown is the *Frid*, drifting her way out of Mariehamn with a cargo of fire logs in 1938, when five 4-masted barques were present. *Tempora mutantur!*

* Not to be confused either with the Norwegian jaegt or jagt.
† The term galleass has had different connotations in different ages and different countries. Usually the fore is the taller mast, carrying the mainsail. The craft illustrated were, properly, schooners.

164. Galleass FRID.

165. FRID passing the 4-masted barque L'AVENIR in Mariehamn.

166. FRID, *viewed from her quarter.*

167. *Galleasses in Stockholm.*

168. *In full storm, the* POMMERN*'s foresail is fast, and she runs under lower topsails only.*

129

Built in 1892 for Laeisz's 'Flying P' line, the *Pisagua* was a magnificent 4-masted barque of 2852 tons with a midship island, but still with the single spanker, since the Germans had not yet adopted the double gaffs at that date. She ran to and from the West Coast of South America in the nitrate trade until 3.55 a.m. on March 16th, 1911 when, running home from Mejillones with a cargo of saltpetre on a clear night at some 10 knots with a southerly wind, she sighted a steamer, which proved to be the P. & O. liner *Oceana* (built in 1887).

The *Oceana* was bound from Tilbury towards Bombay with passengers, silver specie, etc. She sighted the *Pisagua*'s green light and the barque burnt a blue flare in warning. The two vessels were almost on opposite courses, the sailing ship being about two points on the steamer's port bow, when the *Oceana*'s officer gave the order "Port 5°". At this moment, her Channel pilot, who was being carried to the Nab, came on the bridge and asked the chief officer what he was doing. (This was the time of the old helm orders.) He put the helm hard aport. The *Pisagua* had seen the *Oceana*, which was making $14\frac{1}{2}$ knots, six miles away. It was her right of way, as a sailing ship, and she correctly kept both course and speed.

When the P. & O. chief officer was asked at the subsequent court of enquiry for an explanation of his action, he said that he "should have liked to see if the other ship intended to take any action," and "That he should have liked to see what that action was to be before taking any action." This statement, to most seamen, can only cause deep mystification, since he admitted knowledge of the Rule of the Road. The two ships should have passed starboard to starboard, but the *Oceana* crossed the *Pisagua*'s bow and was cut down. Some lives were lost, and the third officer's boat started for the shore without orders.

This occurred south and west of the Royal Sovereign, the cross-Channel steamer *Sussex* taking off the liner's passengers and some of the crew. Tugs took her in tow, but she sank off Beachy Head at 10.00 a.m.

The 'P' ship's bowsprit was bent back and her fore topgallant rigging was in disarray but, with two tugs, she reached Dover later in the day.

130

169. *PISAGUA in the tidal basin at Dover, after discharging her cargo into the s.s. MAGDALENA BLUMENTHAL.*

170. *Ships constantly passed through the Straits of Dover. The Danish PAX, finally broken up in 1920, had always been a smart barque, both as the Norwegian FREYA and, previously, as the BUTTERMERE, owned in Whitehaven.*

171. *Inevitably, with such heavy traffic, there were collisions, and many vessels put into Dover for repair like this barque, believed to be German, with a hole in her bow and a twisted fore-foot.*

172. *Partially dismasted; yards broken and with her top-hamper in disarray, this brigantine took shelter in Dover. A man at the lower mast cap prepares to send down the wreckage.*

173. *The BESSIE of Salcombe was built in 1879 as a 2-masted fore-and-aft schooner, owned in Truro. About the turn of the century she was lengthened and rigged as a 3-masted topsail schooner. Here, in Dover, her bowsprit is gone and her stem torn clean from the bow.*

174. C. B. PEDERSEN in tow and making sail.

Latterly, square-riggers took steam from or to Dover when arriving or leaving the London River. The *C. B. Pedersen*, a Swedish sail-training ship, had previously been the *Elsa Ölander* after being the Norwegian *Ferm*, but had originally been one of the few 4-masters built in Italy as the *Emmanuele Accame*. In more affluent days, ships would be towed to or from Beachy Head or the Start. There were no daylight morse lamps in those days and semaphore was not much practised. Thus, if a master towing in the Channel wished to continue to—say—the Lizard, a board or hatch cover would be lowered over the bow with the message chalked upon it. The tug would give two hoots as a signal that the message was understood. It was crude, but it worked! The *C. B. Pedersen* was sunk by a steamer in 1935.

175. A picture which tells its own story. Being one big shell between her forward and after bulkheads, a sailing ship hit between these points would sink like a stone unless loaded with timber.

176. *Off the South Foreland—'O, Peaceful England'.*

177. *Topsail schooner EUPHEMIA with a ketch and schooner.*

179. *Watkins' famous old tug ARCADIA tows the PONAPE to sea. Sailing ships would set sail with a fair wind to help the tug.*

178. *ABRAHAM RYDBERG comes up to her tug off Dover.*

180. Luggers ANNE and LOUISA on the beach at Kingsdown, 1900.

For the shiplover in the days of sail, few places in the British Isles could have equalled in fascination that historic anchorage known as The Downs which lies off Deal within the treacherous Goodwin Sands of evil memory; ever-shifting shoals that provide either a safe roadstead or an appalling death-trap according to what the weather may be doing, and which a sudden shift of wind can in a moment convert from the one extreme to the other.

Here it was that ships outward bound were wont to lie at anchor waiting for a fair slant down Channel and, if in the night an easterly wind should spring up, dawn would disclose an anchorage completely empty where five, six or even seven hundred ships had been riding when the sun went down. It was to cater for the multifarious needs of this shipping, from supplying provisions to landing passengers or providing pilots, and this in all weathers, fair or foul, that the magnificent beach boats of Deal were developed.

The largest of these were the world-famous Deal luggers that a century ago could be seen berthed side by side, like the *Louisa* and the *Anne*, DL 14, in Plate 180, but then in their dozens, cheek by jowl, in

140

181. Kingsdown lugger ANNE, DL 14, under sail, 1897.

their stations at Deal, Walmer and Kingsdown. Standard practice was to chock them up above high water mark, facing the sea, at the top of the shingle beach. This was so steep that the luggers could be launched from it, fully manned and with reefed sails ready to hoist, even in the teeth of an onshore gale. Sliding down greased planks, locally known as 'woods', they would gather such momentum that, if the moment to launch had been well chosen, with their great weight they would crash through the first breaker and be under sail, clawing off the lee shore before the next heavy sea could knock them back. In this way, anchors and chains weighing up to seven tons would be successfully ferried off to some ship that had parted her cable or was otherwise in dire need of assistance.

Originally rigged as 3-masted luggers, by the middle of the nineteenth century the centre mast had been taken out, to allow more unobstructed space amidships where such heavy loads could be carried and, very important, unloaded with least difficulty. Thus the normal rig of the luggers became that of the *Anne*, shown under sail in Plate 181. It should, however, be noted that she was not quite a

182. Walmer lugger RENOWN, beaching, 1894.

typical lugger, having an extension to her hull aft forming what is known as a 'lute' stern, as distinct from the more usual upright transom of the *Louisa*. The big Deal luggers, clinker-built of elm and some 38 ft. 6 ins. in length, were divided into two classes. The larger were the 'forepeakers', which were decked forward as far aft as the mast, providing a cuddy with bunks where the crew could get some rest when away down Channel, seeking pilotage work, for example, perhaps involving a week or more at sea. The cat boats, or 'cats', similarly rigged but slightly smaller, were undecked and had no more than a portable 'caboose' between the fore and main thwarts, beneath which three or four men could lie down under cover, but otherwise lacking all comfort.

When coming in to the land, a lugger would be sailed straight for the beach and, just before touching, the helm was put down so that

142

183. Deal galley punt, second class.

she took the shingle beach broadside on, as the Walmer lugger *Renown* is doing in Plate 182. The end of a wire from her shore capstan was passed through a hole in the after end of her keel, and she was then hauled up stern first, men laying woods in her path to provide a portable slipway over which she could be dragged. Once in position, she was again chocked up, facing the sea and ready to launch.

For the more general day by day work of tending on the shipping, smaller punts were employed, of which the most numerous were the galley punts. These were open clinker-built boats rigged with a single tall mast stepped nearly amidships, on which was set a single square-headed lug sail. Like the big luggers, they were divided into two classes. Of these, the larger, or first class, galley punts were some 27 ft. to 30 ft. in overall length, and one of the shorter boats is seen

143

184. Deal galley punt, first class, approaching the shore.

approaching the shore under sail in Plate 183. An unusual feature to be noted is that, in addition to the reef cringles spaced evenly on luff and leech in line with the rows of reef points, there were additional intermediate eyelets worked into the bolt-rope, known as 'stakens'. These allowed a half reef to be taken in quickly without the need to tie the points, so that the speed under sail could be regulated to a nicety

144

185. Kingsdown Foresail and Mizzen punt.

to meet any requirement. Although not so big as the luggers, the first class galley punts were still quite full-bodied enough to be used as weight-carriers, whereas the second class were intended more for such lighter tasks as landing and taking off pilots, passengers or letters in finer conditions. One of these, just arrived on the beach, is seen in Plate 184.

186. *Foresail and Mizzen punt at Deal. What was the special occasion? A new boat perhaps: the builder and proud owner aft, and the hands for'ard.*

Coming further down the scale were the foresail-and-mizzen punts, used largely for such general purposes as inshore fishing; and examples of these are seen in Plates 185 and 186.

Today, all the luggers and galley punts have long since disappeared. Perhaps their epitaph was best expressed by the boatmen's famous parson, the Rev. T. S. Treanor, when he wrote:— "While ships are parting from their anchors and flying signals of distress, the luggers supplying their wants or putting pilots on board wheel and swoop round them like sea birds on the wing."

Further down Channel, the boats working from the beaches of Sussex were used principally for fishing, and were registered either at Rye, for those of Hastings, or at Newhaven for Brighton and Worthing craft. Unlike the Deal boats, they stood on the beach with

146

187.   45 NN—a sturdy south coast lugger, registered at Newhaven.

their bows pointing inland, and were invariably launched stern first. A good example of a Sussex lute stern is seen in the old photograph, Plate 188, of a Worthing beach boat. She is particularly interesting in that she is fully yawl rigged, with gaff mainsail, yard topsail, foresail, jib on a long bowsprit and standing lug mizzen. This would suggest that she was more likely to be used for taking visitors for 'trips on the briny', at least in summer time, than for the more serious business of fishing. Another old photograph, Plate 187, shows a Newhaven registered clinker-built lugger, considerably larger than the Worthing craft, and having the more modern short elliptical counter which was gradually coming into fashion at the time. The photograph may well have been taken at Brighton. She is a fine sturdy looking craft, well able to take care of herself in the short Channel seas of the home waters where she had to earn her living in almost all weathers.

188.   Worthing beach boat in 1871.

Both Plates 186 and 188 are interesting sidelights on social history. The former, taken by Amos of Dover, shows the implicit class distinction in the gap between the owner and his hands, while the latter shows the bathing machines which were then the height of fashion, begun in the 1790's by King George III with his own 'right royal and cumbersome affair'.*

*Note: At Weymouth where:— 'many folk come daily into the town to see His Majesty and the Court bathing in the sea water half a furlong out from the shore.' (Randall: From the North Foreland to Penzance, 1908)

148

189. *Trawler SEAFARER heading into Brixham.*

190. *GUESS AGAIN making 12 knots in the annual regatta. This Brixham Mule— a smaller type of trawler, was immortalised by Arthur Briscoe in his etchings aboard her. Impressed by the hardship of the men's lot, one feels that here they must be experiencing the higher moments of life!*

191. Off Plymouth Hoe. Trawlers; lugger and a Tamar barge.

How long ago trawl fishing began at Brixham is not accurately known, but there is contemporary evidence that about the year 1770 there were seven trawlers working from the port, and that by 1833 their number had increased to some 112 first class smacks, ranging from 30 to 40 tons. Their influence, however, was out of all proportion to the size of their home port, for trawl fishing from Ramsgate, Lowestoft, the River Humber and in Dublin Bay was all started by trawlers migrating from Brixham and taking their methods of fishing with them. Up to the year 1882, the Brixham trawlers were all cutter-rigged 'long-boomers', but from then onwards the ketch rig began to find favour, and the ultimate development of the typical Brixham trawler is seen in the *Revive*, BM 134, photographed with her big 'tow foresail' set and drawing well, racing at one of the regattas at the end of the First World War.

Like the Brixham craft, the Plymouth trawlers were originally 'long-boomers', but in due course that also changed to the ketch rig seen in the trawler PH 47 lying at anchor with sail set off Plymouth Hoe, identified by the tower of Smeaton's old Eddystone lighthouse in

150

192. *Brixham trawler REVIVE, BM 134, racing after the First World War.*

193. A Cornish stone barge sailing past Plymouth trawlers home from sea.

Plate 191. Another Plymouth trawler is sailing along under the land, while taking a fair wind up towards Devonport is one of the smaller Tamar type Cornish stone barges, similar to the *Shamrock* that is now being restored by the National Trust for preservation and exhibition at Cotehele, near Calstock. In the further distance is one of the two-masted Plymouth luggers under sail.

More of these luggers appear berthed bows-on to the Fish Quay at the Barbican in Plate 194, where they may be distinguished from the Plymouth hookers in the foreground, which are cutter-rigged, by the fact that these all have mast-heads painted white. A somewhat similar old photograph, also probably representing the Barbican, appears as Plate 193. This is interesting in that it shows the harbour well packed with trawlers, while running between them, deeply laden, is a Cornish stone barge of the sea-going type, rather larger than that

152

194. *Off the Barbican, Plymouth. Hookers in the foreground, luggers beyond.*

195. Mounts Bay lugger and old style of cutter-rigged trading smack.

in Plate 191, to which reference was made above.

Proceeding on into Cornwall, one finds a significant difference in hull form east and west of the Lizard. In the east, exemplified by the Mevagissey luggers of Plate 196, transom sterns prevail, because ports are generally spacious natural harbours, like Fowey and Falmouth, or even artificial harbours such as Mevagissey, which are comparatively easy of access, and where craft can lie afloat, at least on arrival. Further west, however, they are small, artificial, and dry out, like Penzance and Mousehole, and there double-ended craft, like the Mounts Bay lugger of Plate 195, are almost universal. The reason is that, with square-sterned boats berthed bows-on to the quay, an incoming craft is faced with an impenetrable wall of transoms whereas, with sharp sterns, a row of wedge-shaped openings awaits her, into any one of which she can slide as easily as a woman's foot

196. *Mevagissey luggers setting out for the fishing grounds.*

197. Counter-sterned Mounts Bay lugger, built on East Coast drifter lines.

slips into her shoe. A tight squeeze, maybe, but that is all, and no damage is suffered. It was also possible to pack far more double-ended craft into a small space—witness a tin of sardines!

There were exceptions, like the lugger 55 PZ of Plate 197, but she was a copy of a Yarmouth drifter, and not of Cornish origin. Of additional interest in Plate 195 is the cutter-rigged cargo smack, a real old-timer of a type once common in these waters. Here, seen flying light, note the loose-footed mainsail and the high bulwarks on a hull like half a walnut shell that had grown a heavy counter.

156

198. *PONAPE running through a fresh Trade, bound towards Falmouth for orders.*

199. CHAMPIGNY being towed into Carrick Roads.

Falmouth is not only a beautiful harbour, but a most remarkable one, since it has retained its position as a busy port for many years yet, apart from handling fruit and mails in its early days, has seldom dealt with cargo to any extent. In virtue of its geographical position it became, with Queenstown, one of the main ports at which sailing ships called after long passages to receive their orders for discharging port and, for much the same reason, became the haven of so many vessels which had suffered damage in the Channel or beyond.

Plate 199 shows the beautiful French 4-masted barque *Champigny* arriving in Carrick Roads, to await her orders. Built in 1902 at Havre for the Societé des Long-Courriers, she had a gross tonnage of 3112 and a net tonnage of 2778, having the long (115 ft.) poop and foc's'le head of the French ships of the 'Bounty' period. Sold to the Finland line as a sail-training ship in 1922, she had the distinction of being the last square-rigger to be dismasted off the Horn, and was condemned as a hulk in Port Stanley, being then the *Fennia*.

158

200. HERZOGIN CECILIE leaving Falmouth.

This well-known vessel needs little introduction, since she has received more than her share of sea literature. Built by Rickmers of Bremerhaven for the North German Lloyd as a sail-training ship in 1902, apart from a dismasting on her maiden voyage, she gave a good account of herself. After the 1914-18 war she was allocated to France but bought and run by Capt. Gustaf Erikson of Mariehamn until she was most lamentably stranded near Salcombe in 1936.

She is hoisting her mizzen royal in this picture but, with her hull all being painted white and with her double spankers, she was not, perhaps, as pleasing to the eye as some of her contemporaries. The double spanker arrangement became a German foible, although the evidence is that it was not, as is commonly believed, a German idea, since the two barques named *Gwydyr Castle*, owned by R. Thomas of Liverpool, carried this arrangement of double gaffs before any German ships. Despite its advantages, it does not seem that British masters or owners pursued the idea. Few new ideas were welcomed!

159

201. INVERAVON, ex JOHN COOK, off Falmouth.

Built in 1889 by J. Bigger for Mitchell's of Londonderry, of 1879 tons, the *John Cook* passed to Stuart Bros. of Glasgow and then to George Milne's 'Inver' line in 1909. Leaving London for Melbourne on Christmas Day, she had to beat against strong sou'westerly gales to the Lizard, when she encountered squalls of hurricane force. The main topmast backstays carried away and, on the next roll, the topmast came down, bringing with it the mizzen royal and part of that topgallant mast. After five days a tug picked her up and brought her to Falmouth where this picture was taken. She was two months refitting, and went missing between Callao and Puget Sound in 1913.

The *Sorine*, of only 398 tons, was built in Denmark in 1891. Bound from Cuba towards Falmouth, she was sighted in 36°N, 48°W, dismasted and riding to a sea-anchor, with her rudder gone. Her master, Capt. Andersen, refused assistance and, after being placed on the Overdue list, she finally arrived. She was lost in ice in 1910 or 1911 when chartered to the Hudson Bay Company.

202. *The SORINE finally arrived under jury-rig.*

203. *The Arendal barque ZEUS, built in 1869 of 391 tons, lying in Falmouth after being struck by lightning—a cause for speculation with such a name!*

204. BONA racing.

Apart from being a great port for merchant sail, Falmouth was naturally a great yachting centre. Those who recall Arthur Briscoe's sad little sketch of the yacht *Bona* hard and fast on the rock in the Helford River which is now known as 'Bona Rock', may be interested to see her racing off Falmouth in all her pride. The yachts of that generation had a beauty of sail plan sadly lacking in their modern counterparts. Whether in yachts or merchantmen, beauty has been abandoned for a sheer, ruthless efficiency.

Devotees of Briscoe may also like to see pictures of the Falmouth pilot cutter *F8* which he portrayed so splendidly. The Falmouth cutters seldom cruised beyond the confines of the Lizard, unlike those from, say, Bristol, which might be found soliciting business very far afield, whether beyond Malin Head or well out in the Western Approaches. Falmouth was a splendid haven, but the surrounding rock-bound coasts took a tremendous toll of fine sailing ships. Many such pictures are well-known, but a few are reproduced here. Only a small proportion of such ships survived.

205. *Falmouth pilot cutter F8 passing H.M.S. BACCHANTE and H.M.S. VENGEANCE.*

206. *The Lizard, seen along the deck of the same Falmouth pilot cutter.*

207. *Tug standing by the barque CHILI off the Lizard.*

One of A. D. Bordes' barques, the *Chili*, built for them by W. B. Thompson of Glasgow in 1885, was of 1318 tons gross. On Feb. 12th, 1912 she almost ran ashore on the Lizard in fog, the steam drifter *Maud* (in the foreground) having done so a few days before. The Lizard lifeboat is passing a line to the waiting tug in the picture. The barque was sunk by U-54 in 1917, homeward bound with nitrate from Iquique to Nantes.

A year after her launch in 1895, the *Aberfoyle* was found drifting off Tasmania after her master had been washed overboard and her mate had committed suicide. She became well known running to 'Frisco and Puget Sound but, in 1910, became the Norwegian *Hansy*, of Frederikstad. In November the next year she missed stays off the Lizard in bad weather with a cargo of timber and pig iron, with the result seen in Plate 208.

Many ships piled up on the Scillies. The *Queen Mab* was one, but the weather was kind and she was brought into Penzance.

208. HANSY, *wrecked near the Lizard.*

209. *QUEEN MAB in Penzance. (Later the Norwegian ALFA and Swedish SENTA.)*

210. FAVELL off Falmouth in June, 1927.

Last of the Bristol-built square-riggers and constructed under a covered shed, being launched in 1895 for C. Hill of that port, the *Favell* was a cargo-carrying sail-training ship for the Finland line at the time this picture was taken. Seldom making noteworthy passages, she was one of the last deep-watermen to cross single topgallants. Of course, many of the modern school-ships are so rigged, but they are always so high in the water, and their decks so full of various erections, boats and rafts, that they can never equal the appearance of the *Favell* in Plate 210, despite the fact that she has not yet overhauled her buntlines or trimmed her yards to a nicety. Painted black in her final years, which was not an improvement aesthetically, she was broken up in 1934. Her odd name derived from Miss Favell Hill, of her original owner's family.

166

211. *The 442-ton Spanish barque TULA built in Ferrol in 1882 sails prettily up the Channel. Not using her gaff, she sets a small jib-headed spanker.*

212. *Originally the Liverpool 4-masted barque AUSTRASIA, the GUSTAV was owned by Wm. Miller of Hamburg in 1912 when she went ashore off Portscatho. Salved, she was owned after the war by Vinnen Gebr. and Hermann Engels, ending her life as Gustaf Erikson's MELBOURNE when run down by a tanker off Queenstown.*

213. German brigantine becalmed.

With her deck cargo carried right aft, one might wonder about the trim of this little brigantine, although she looks to be all right. Certainly little effort is required in such a calm, but a deck cargo of this nature does not make for easier working of the little vessel. Pretty craft like these used to proliferate the short seas.

Arriving off Penzance in happier circumstances than the *Queen Mab*, about her lawful occasions, is the Norwegian barque *Naja* of 414 tons. Built in Arendal in 1872, she was sold to Sweden in 1905. A vessel often came to anchor with only her upper topsails set, since they could be lowered and taken in very quickly.

The *Sylphiden*, a wooden barque built in Grimstad in 1873 of 398 tons, is just about to let go her anchor. She was condemned in 1898. Her windmill pump is spinning and slightly out of focus. These two ships were both contemporary Norwegian-built barques, and it is interesting to compare the differences in arrangements of their buntlines, the *Naja* clewing to the quarters, the *Sylphiden*, on the other hand, to her yard-arms.

168

214. *NAJA coming to anchor off Penzance.*

215. *SYLPHIDEN arriving off Penzance.*

216. PONAPE—wind aft, with staysails and spanker fast. 1935.

Of the eight 4-masted barques built in Italy, one was the attractive *Regina Elena* in 1903 at Riva Trigosa for Pietro Milesi and of 2365 tons gross. In 1911 she passed to the Hamburg 'P' line who lost her after the war, and she came successively under the house-flags of Sir James Bell as the *Bellhouse*, Monsens of Tonsberg with the same name, and then under Hugo Lundquist and Gustaf Erikson with her Laeisz name of *Ponape*. Nothing is better than the sensation of a fine 4-master with a fair wind. In Plate 216 the wind is aft, and the staysails and spanker are fast (though the boom is not hauled amidships). In Plate 140 the wind has hauled a little to the quarter, and she has ideal sailing conditions. An attractive vessel, she was broken up in 1936.

170

217.   FLYING FOAM at Par.

218. Topsail schooners in Mounts Bay.

Penzance did not cater for large vessels, but on occasions its harbour could be literally packed with coastal schooners. Here three are passing St. Michael's Mount, as similar as three peas in a pod except that one has a wheel-house. No doubt others were in sight, but not caught by the camera.

The *Flying Foam* was built in Jersey, C.I. in 1879, but was owned in Bridgwater and trading right up to the winter of 1935/6 when she drove ashore at Llandudno in a gale. Mainly in the china clay trade she was often in the Thames. Seen on the mud at Par, Plate 217 gives a good idea of the hull form of these attractive craft.

Latterly, she was under the command of Capt. Slee, who still wore gold earrings, and who also had the ketch *Henrietta* (Plate 220). This little schooner managed to avoid the degradation of being cut down aloft and given an engine, like so many of her kind.

172

219. ENIGMA.

Built in Calcutta of teak, copper-fastened and with a broadside of 4 guns and two swivels, and a crew of about 100 when launched in 1845 for the opium trade, this schooner had a romantic beginning. After some years on the China coast, she left Calcutta for home with general cargo, but put into Peel, I.o.M. with weather damage. Being auctioned then, she was owned in the Isle of Man and put in the Spanish and Baltic trades but, changing hands again in the 1870's, she was employed bringing coal to the Isle of Man. In 1922 she went missing in the winter gales but, despite being sister of the *Torrington*, which is said to have been a catalyst to the clippers, many a bluff coaster could outsail her.

The little *Jane*, of 100 tons, was even older, being built in Pwllheli in 1827, and owned in Caernarvon when Plate 221 was taken in the Mersey as she passed the coaster *Dalegarth*. Note her stern!

173

220. LA REVANCHE, ketch HENRIETTA and CARMENTA.

Leaving Newlyn on a calm day in 1926, on the left is *La Revanche*, one of the many 'roller-topsail' schooners, registered at Hennebout and, of 131 tons, built at Paimpol in 1915. There were hundreds of these distinctive French schooners, with the roller gear which enabled the sail to be reefed or furled from the deck. Although patent reefing gear had been tried, with varying success, it had been shown that it only worked well with relatively small sails. Only one or two British schooners were ever rigged in this manner which, again, may be a measure of British distrust of new improvements. The French used it both on their short-sea and Iceland schooners. In effect, the sail was rolled onto a small yard rotated from a bigger yard above it, by tackles led to the deck.

The ketch is the well-known St. Austell coaster *Henrietta*, while the *Carmenta* was built in 1879 as the *Ellen Kirstone* at Truro and, at the time of the picture, was owned by A. E. Tope of South Shields.

221. *The old schooner JANE in the Mersey.*

222. BROOKLANDS, ex SUSAN VITTERY.

Built at Dartmouth as the 2-masted schooner *Susan Vittery* in 1860, this trim little schooner may have originally been in the Mediterranean soft fruit trade, which demanded speed with so perishable a cargo. Of 138 tons and 100 feet in length, she was bigger than most of the vessels so engaged. Owned by Vittery of Brixham, she passed to H. A. Hawksley of Mevagissey when the Vitterys ceased ship-owning and continued in the Newfoundland salt trade, in which she was by then engaged with her sisters. Generally she sailed deep-water for many years but, in 1923, was re-rigged as a 3-master and is seen here getting along very well with her flying foresail set. She survived into the Second World War. It is generally true that these little ships maintained greater continuity with their crews, who maintained better ties with home, than the deep-watermen.

176

223. The UNITED SERVICE tows a Padstow schooner out of Yarmouth as the REAPER tows in Kircaldy and Fraserburgh fifies.

There has grown up a myth that the coasting schooners belonged almost exclusively to the West Country. Nothing could be further from the truth, although it is undeniable that this area played its part both in their building and in ownership. There were vast fleets in Wales: schooners running down the East Coast with coal and, indeed, they could be found in almost all harbours, both big and small, in this country and elsewhere.

There were, of course, variations in the actual rig, but, when the situation is reviewed in retrospect, it becomes clearer and clearer that they provided some of the best basic training, and that their men were far better equipped in certain aspects of seamanship and in ship-handling, particularly in close navigation and in confined waters, than their deep-sea brethren.

The *Irish Minstrel* had been built as a brigantine in 1879, and was the last vessel afloat to have been launched in Dundalk. Latterly she was rigged as a 3-masted schooner with a whale-back wheelhouse and, although she had a number of owners, was long registered at Connah's Quay, usually loading china clay or coal.

Considering the dates when they were built—and the *Englishman* saw the light in Glasson Dock in 1864, one might suppose them to be very long lived craft but, of course, we are dealing with those which, by chance or fortune, survived to the end. This schooner found herself being shelled by a U-boat in the first war and, being utterly defenceless, was virtually a sitting duck. Luckily for her, help arrived on the scene and she survived another seven years until she foundered on the Pembrokeshire coast in 1923.

One of the last schooners in trade was the *Mary Miller*, of 119 tons, which was built by Rogers in Carrickfergus in 1881, and first owned by J. Fisher and Sons of Barrow who had, at that time, some 42 vessels in the coastal trade, although some did sometimes trade abroad. Latterly she was frequently seen in the Thames with china clay, when under the management of C. W. Couch of St. Austell.

Unhappily, in the last days of sail, many of the schooners lost their square topsails (though not all had them), and often became rigged down and fitted with auxiliary engines to cope with the inexorable march of 'Progress'.

225. *ENGLISHMAN.*

224. *IRISH MINSTREL.*

226. MARY MILLER.

180

227. Seen in company with a big ketch, the *CUMBERLAND LASSIE*, built at Amlwch in 1874, was a collier-schooner well-known on the East coast running coals from Hartlepool to Dover and Folkestone.

228. WATERWITCH.

Although originally a brig this little barquentine of 207 tons achieved fame by being the last square-rigged vessel flying the Red Ensign. Rumour had it that, when she was launched at Poole in 1871 by Meadows, her timbers were taken from an old line-of-battleship. On occasions, she showed quite a turn of speed, and another tale of her is that there was, at one time, a hole in her after deck into which her one-legged skipper braced his wooden leg in bad weather!

She is believed to have traded both to the West Indies and to the Mediterranean in the days of her youth, and was certainly in the Newfoundland stockfish trade but, after the first war, she was mainly running from the Cornish china clay ports to the North-East coast. She also had a long spell as an East coast collier, and was converted to a barquentine in 1884. After being laid up for three years, she was sold to Esthonia in 1939 for £400, but deteriorated in the war.

229.   *WATERWITCH at anchor.*

183

At first sight one might suppose that the ketch *Charlotte Sophia*, built in Portsmouth in 1876 and in the centre of Plate 230, was lying between two conventional topgallant-yard schooners. The *Zebrina*, nearest the camera, is far from being a conventional vessel, since she was one of a number, varying between the odd barque, brig and a number of schooners, which were built with barge hulls, since they could stand up in normal circumstances without ballast and could also negotiate shallow harbours and rivers at neap tides.

The *Zebrina* is generally said to have been barquentine-rigged originally. Of course, a barquentine does not carry a fore and aft fore lower, but staysails between main and fore, and in this picture her fore-yard is that of a schooner, though it *does* have a square sail bent to it. (Schooners normally set flying foresails, from the deck, see Plate 222.) All these barge-built craft had normal barge lee-boards, except for the *Zebrina* which was originally built at Whitstable by H. H. Gann in 1873 for the River Plate, where she remained for eight years. Oak-built and copper-fastened, she measured 185 tons gross and was 109.1 feet in length by 23.9 by 9.9 feet in depth. She did not have fidded topgallant-masts and her fiddle bow, rather like a ram with a sharp inward rake, is not immediately obvious in the picture.

On her return from the Plate she traded coastwise and short-seas very profitably, but became the source of some speculation during the war since, when bound from South Wales towards St. Brieuc with a cargo of coal, she was found ashore just south of Cherbourg. Everything aboard was intact, but there were no crew, and they have never been seen from that day to this. Being war-time, it has been suggested that her crew might have been taken prisoners by an enemy submarine which was about to sink the ship but, before she could do so, was attacked and sunk with all hands. If this were so, one might suppose that her attacker might at least have reported—if not salved—the *Zebrina*. The weather was fair at the time, and the incident remains one of the unsolved mysteries of the sea.

She was salved, but given an auxiliary and rigged as a schooner. Later, after a period as a hulk in Ramsgate, she went to sea under almost full power, but finally her cargo caught fire and, putting in to the Solent, she never left again.

230. *ZEBRINA ahead of CHARLOTTE SOPHIA.*

231. GOLDFINCH of Faversham.

Named not for the bird, but for her owner and builder, J. M. Goldfinch of Faversham, the *Goldfinch* was built in 1894 as a schooner-barge with square topsails, and could carry 265 tons at a pinch. Later she was converted to a ketch without square-sails, but these were restored. She does have lee-boards and, when last heard of, was in the Georgetown sugar trade in the Caribbean.

The barque on page 191 was the first *Kalliope*, in the fleet of B. Wencke Sohne of Hamburg, built in 1876 of 1115 tons. In 1888 she was sold to Merrem & La Porte of Amsterdam as the *Anna Herbertha* and in 1894 was managed by K. Bruusgaard of Drammen, foundering at sea in 1912. The most significant thing in Plate 236 are the railway lines. As the ditch at Suez and the cuts and locks of Panama did much to kill the deep-sea sailing ship, so the railway tolled the knell of coasters all over the world. Before its advent, small craft were to be found on open beaches and up muddy creeks all round the coasts, since these were the main means of transport. The railway doomed these vessels more surely than the advent of the steam coaster.

232.   The *CHARLES JAMES* of Portmadoc, built in Pwllheli in 1877, seen in the Mersey.   (Note the sailing ships in the docks.)

233. RAYMOND.

It is difficult for anyone today to imagine the sights which might be seen when a host of vessels left the Downs: the Mersey, the Bristol Channel, or perhaps Mounts Bay and many other areas, after a prolonged period of head-wind or bad weather. Not only would the number of craft be beyond belief, but they would range through every rig and type seen in this book, from large square-riggers to the smallest ketches and cutters.

Barquentines were commonly seen, and rather bigger than the schooners. One of the last to survive was the *Raymond*, originally built on Prince Edward Island in 1876 and, after a period engaged in the Newfoundland trade based on New Quay, in Wales, she spent over twenty years running out of Whitstable before being owned in Poole. She, too, survived a submarine attack in the first war, and finally became a stationary training ship, the *Lady Quirk*, at Chelsea.

188

234. *About her lawful occasions—the ketch PENGUIN of Porlock Weir on the hard at Lynmouth.*

235. CERES.

The ketch *Ceres* became a legend on account of her sheer longevity. Built at Salcombe in 1811, she is believed to have started her career carrying stores to North Spain for Wellington's army in the Peninsular War. If this cannot be proven, it is likely enough.

In 1852, when 41 years old, she was bought by Henry Petherick of Bude, (her third owner), and she ran for this family for the next eighty-four years, trading all round the British coast, until she finally foundered near Appledore in 1936, after earning her keep continuously for *125* years! A staunch craft indeed, particularly since coastal craft tend to suffer more stresses than deep-watermen.

236. *MAGDALENA and the railway lines.*

237. *WORRY NOT, built at Clymping in 1910, alongside another ketch at Littlehampton.*

238. Turkish caique.

The rig of this small Turkish coaster speaks for itself. If she is at all unusual, it is because she carries a square foresail. Although by no means unique, most of these craft confined their square configuration to the topsail. Whilst the rig may, at first sight, seem to be 'all arms and legs', it was nevertheless efficient. The word 'caique' has different connotations in different countries, and the vessel on the hard in Plate 239, also Turkish, strikes a more popular conception, though the vessel above is the true 'caique'. Almost all countries developed their own local types and rigs.

The variety of junks, both on the coast and in the rivers of China, would alone fill many thick tomes, since the types are legion. All are essentially luggers with a high-built poop, an overhanging bow and

239. *Turkish caiques on the hard.*

240. *Salt junk near Hong Kong.*

241. Light salt junk, reefed down.

hulls which, if sometimes apparently ungainly, are generally fine below the waterline. They can have anything from one to five masts, raking different ways and each rigged with the Chinese lug—a balanced sail extended by battens, each of which leads to a sheet led to an outrigger over the stern which enables the sail to be hauled quite flat when close to the wind. The junk type has remained virtually unchanged for long centuries and can sail well off the wind though, often with no keel, it seldom works well to windward.

194

242. Bisquine at St. Servan, 1900.

The juxtaposition of the bisquine and the junk is not entirely accidental. Both have their masts raking different ways, which presents a rather bizarre appearance, and both are rigged with lug sails. The bisquine normally has her foremast stepped right in the eyes and has a short bowsprit and may be of two or three masts, the larger ones being 30 or 40 tons. It must not be confused with the chasse-marée, which normally only carried a topsail on the main and was alternatively known as the 'lougre'. The chaloupe, which used to be found along the Biscay coast, was very similar, deriving from the chasse-marée.

Mostly used for fishing, the type, rather like the junk, had not changed for some seven centuries, and the chasse-marées would often be seen in British Channel ports and doubtless influenced the Beer fishermen, which had a not dissimilar rig, although not setting topsails above the high peaked lower lugs. The bisquine's mainsail was normally a dipping lug—the others were standing.

195

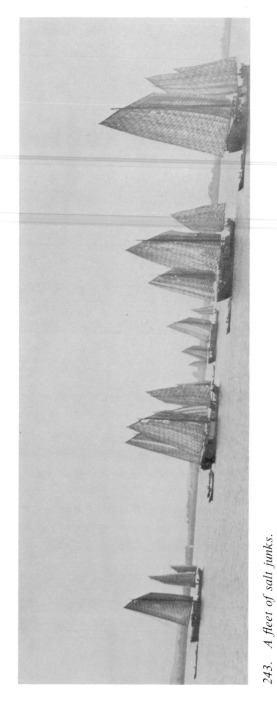

243. *A fleet of salt junks.*

244. *Bisquines off Cancale, 1900.*

245, 246.   *Bisquines off Cancale, 1900.*

246.

248. *Calais bisquines working out of harbour past the Dover to Calais cross-Channel packets.*

249.   Terre-Neuvas in St. Malo, about 1900.

Whilst around Brittany we should consider the Breton fleet of Grand-Bankers—the fleet which put out each year with dories stacked on deck and which were then put out with hand-lines to catch cod—two men to each dory. The French had been engaged in this activity certainly since the sixteenth century, if not before, and Louis XIV was sufficiently interested to issue edicts for the regulation of the trade. The more modern methods did not come into effect until the late 1850's but, although many think of the fleet in terms of the barquentines which will follow in these pages, or the roller-topsail two-masted schooners (similar to *La Revanche*, though bigger, Plate 220) which mainly fished the Iceland Banks, up to and after the turn of the century, the fleet was much more variegated, as this picture shows.

There were barques of varying sizes, brigs like *La Tour d'Auvergne* (Plate 252) seen setting sail off St. Malo which was of 178 tons, built in 1878 and finally sunk by a U-boat off Penzance in April, 1917. Like the Portuguese, the French salted down their cod, whilst the fast American and Canadian two-masted schooners raced their's in fresh whenever possible.

199

250.   Another view of the fleet in St. Malo, about 1900.

It is sometimes said that St. Malo has taken upon itself the mantle of the whole age of the French sailing ship—a distinction which might properly belong to the greater deep-water ports such as Nantes or Dunkerque. No Frenchman will under-estimate the sailing of the *Morutiers*—the Cod-fishermen, lying to in that inhospitable expanse of water called the Grand Banks of Newfoundland with the constant bad weather: the ice-cold Labrador Current sweeping down from the Davis Straits; the icebergs and the attendant fog; the danger of ships and dories being run down by passing ships and, withal, the gutting and salting of the fish at night after a long day in the dories. The barque on the opposite page was well named *Sans Peur*. St. Malo, with some of the smaller Breton ports—Roscoff, Paimpol, Féchamp and the like—played the game to the bitter end. The white barquentine in the foreground makes a contrast with the older, painted-port ships beyond, and was one of the fore-runners of the final stage in the development of the Terre-Neuvas.

200

251. Barque *SANS PEUR*, built in 1882 at St. Servan.

252. *LA TOUR D'AUVERGNE off St. Malo, 1900.*

253. *NOTRE DAME DE ST. JOVAN, 320 tons, towing out of St. Malo. She foundered in 1938.*

254. *PERE PIERRE making sail. Built 1920 of 338 tons gross, she was sold in 1938.*

255. *The fleet in St. Malo became almost all 3-masted barquentines. Smaller schooners in the trade generally used the smaller ports.*

256. *CAPITAINE GUYNEMER, built 1918, makes sail after casting off her tug. She was sold to Denmark in 1932, and was of 332 tons. Lost in 1946.*

257. *ERMITE, setting sail.*

Built in 1924 by Lemoine at St. Malo of 335 tons, this barquentine, which was so typical of the year of her building, was lost, like so many more, off the coast of Greenland after springing a leak. Their hulls were subject to many stresses.

On the opposite page, the Grand Banks fisherman *Felicité* has been caught in a flash of sunlight while she was hove-to in bad weather on the Grand Banks. Like most photographs of vessels hove-to in these conditions, the dramatic quality of the situation fails to transmit itself to the camera.

This vessel was built in 1903 by Yvon and Leroux and measured 150 tons. France tends to pride itself on the *nuances* of its language and, indeed, has the word *brigantin* for 'brigantine' but no word for what we term a barquentine. *Goélette*, with various qualifications, means 'schooner', yet the French nautical fraternity refer to all three rigs as *goélettes*, which can make their records confusing. That the *Ermite* is a barquentine and the *Felicité* a brigantine is not in doubt, though both are described as *goélettes* in France.

204

258. *FELICITÉ hove-to on the Grand Banks.*

259. TURENNE leaving Féchamp.

Most of the Terre-Neuvas were built in France, usually along the Breton ports. The *Turenne*, formerly named the *Myrtle*, was one of the few bought in, having been built in 1883 on the Black River, in New Brunswick. One, the *Famalicao* was built in Portugal in 1921 (292 tons), but condemned in 1923 due to the inferior timbers of which she was constructed!

260. *The Terre-Neuve GLOIRE À DIEU about to cast off her tug, outward-bound.*

261. *Note the high pointed bows of the later Bankers. L. to R.:—PORTO, built 1921, 392 tons. VIANA, built 1921 and NAVARIN of 1911. The PORTO was sold to Portugal in 1935 and the NAVARIN sank off Greenland in 1934. She was 287 tons.*

262. *VIANA making her departure. Of 406 tons—one of the largest—she was built at Villa do Condé for the French Cod-Fishing Co. of Féchamp and was registered in the Island of St. Pierre, Miquelon.*

263. *FRANÇOIS CHARLES entering Granvelle.*

Although, latterly, the Bretons were building a fairly standard type of barquentine for the cod-fishery, there was no real magic about the vessels to be used. Clearly, they needed a deck arrangement to cater both for handling dories and for dealing with the fish, and they needed suitable holds for storing the salted cod in tubs. However, in earlier days many older ships were purchased for the trade. The ships may have been laid up in the winter months but the trade was a hard one, and many the vessel whose loss is listed as *'voie d'eau'*.

Thus the little barque *Otra*, built in Kristianssand in 1866, was bought in 1900 and is seen here off Granvelle, re-named *François Charles*. Her dories can be seen stacked abaft her fore-mast.

The pretty little single topsail schooners, with their roller gear, were mainly used on the Iceland fishery, of the type so splendidly described in Pierre Loti's novel *Pêcheur d'Islande*. Both feeding and living conditions in the *Morutiers* were hard, while the loss of men was greater than in almost any other trade.

264. *Brigantine in Ajaccio.*

Not the most beautiful of the many lovely harbours and bays in Corsica, this little brigantine is pretty enough as she lies discharging into a cart hauled by the inevitable Corsican donkeys! Up until this time, the Mediterranean was an extraordinary sea so far as sail was concerned, since it contained such a mixture of the old and the new— the lateen and the square-sail or boom and gaff rig. Marseilles, not such an important deep-water harbour as the French Atlantic and Channel ports, nevertheless might contain almost every sort of rig, ranging from lateen-rigged tartanes to 4-masted barques, and even British coasters.

The Suez Canal, at its eastern end, may have spelled out one of the death-knells of the sailing ship, but the local craft of its own waters had not changed in centuries. The word 'Felucca' is a loose one which has slightly different connotations in different countries.

265. Felucca in the Mahmudia Canal, in Lower Egypt near Kafr el Dauwar.

Usually with two short masts and no headsails or upper sails, it is subject to fluctuations. The felucca in Plate 265 is passing a Gyassa, also illustrated in Plate 266, which term covers a variety of 2- and 3-masted barges of Arabic ancestry which are found in the Nile Delta and in the Suez Canal. Sometimes found at sea, all are lateen-rigged with wall sides and a high bow decked up to the stem-head, which feature must be almost unique. There are short lengths of keel forward and aft on the flat bottom, these being flushed with the bottom amidships. Their object is to provide more protection for the hull when grounding, besides giving more grip on the water. This vessel has a lateen mizzen, though a settee (with a short, square luff) was more common. The moored gyassa in Plate 265 is being passed by a one-masted felucca, as it is generally called, despite its Italian origin, at a good eight knots, for she is making the most of the fair wind.

211

266. Gyassa in the Suez Canal.

This local barge is, in fact, having the benefit of a tow in this picture. Although her sails look as though they had suffered the depredations of moth, the fact remains that craft like this fulfil a very useful existence and can function quite efficiently with such canvas for a long period in the regions in which they are found. In any case, hot sun has a most deleterious effect on canvas, and deep-sea ships always bent their oldest suits of sails in the tropics.

267.   Settee-rigged dhow.

213

268. Sambuk arriving in port.

Once through the Suez Canal, one is in the realm of the dhow, whose influence, in one form or another, extends all down the Red Sea and from—say—Mozambique to India. The study of this type is a very wide one, made the more difficult by the fact that the Arabs do not use the word 'dhow' at all! It seems to have been a European piece of word coinage. It is held to refer to all that vast family of lateen-rigged vessels of these areas, for all have a long overhang forward: a steep rise of floor and large beam, with a raking transom stern. In general terms, the dhows have remained highly successful trading craft for centuries and, indeed, were making ocean voyages long before Western man within his own history. Apart from the odd addition of an internal combustion engine, as if to propitiate the Gods of oil, they have not changed their form at all. They were trading in just the same manner when the Portuguese navigators first sailed round the Cape of Good Hope and made contact with the Arabs there, to find them far

214

269. The form of a dhow's hull.

ahead of European seamen in their navigation, thanks to the superior knowledge of the Arab astronomers, whilst they had had crude compasses long before men on the Atlantic seaboards. Originally built with two skins, the intervening space is filled with a mixture of chunam and an oil they term *galgal*, whilst the same preparation is applied to the outer shell as a deterrent to the teredo: copper sheathing being unknown to them.

There is a tremendous variation in possible sizes. The Arabs themselves generally call the smaller craft of this type *sambuks* and the larger ones *baghlas*, but even these terms are very general and the whole study of these craft would take a lifetime. All have two or three forward-raking masts, and in the bigger craft the handling of the lateen yard presents man-power problems which would make most Western owners blench! Dhows always had a propensity to sail without lights, as much to their own danger as to that of others!

270.   CASSARD, drying sails.

Blown off our course through the Suez Canal and into the Indian Ocean, we shall return to France to illustrate some of their Bounty ships. There is no doubt that the French did have a very fine fleet of deep-water sailing ships which, with the advantage of Government subsidy, was able to compete on better terms with those of other countries at the end of the last century and beginning of this one. Undoubtedly some of their ships were second to none, and we have already seen some of these vessels. Many of their ships were full-riggers or barques, either bald-headed or with royals to a standard plan, and, indeed, there were no less than 31 barques built from one set of plans which were virtually indistinguishable. The Bounty will not be discussed in detail here, but it depended, in some measure, on gross tonnage, which is why so many ships were built with elongated foc's'le heads and poops which became shelter-decked. They were smartly kept and to be found all over the world, trading particularly

216

271. MARGUERITE MIRABAUD wrecked south of Dunedin.

to the West coasts of America, Australia and to New Caledonia.

The *Cassard*, built in 1892 and measuring 2292 tons gross, is shown drying her sails on arrival prior to sending them below. In 1906, when bound from Sydney towards Falmouth for orders, she drove ashore on Bleaker Island in the Falklands in thick weather and a north-easterly gale.

The *Marguerite Mirabaud* was launched ten years later but, one of the Societé des Voiliers Francais' fleet of Havre, she went ashore and became a total loss, rather strangely, south of Dunedin when bound from La Rochelle towards Tahiti in 1907, during foggy weather and bad visibility.

The *Le Carbet* was built by Birrel Stenhouse for W. Nichol of Liverpool as the *Bothnia* in 1878 and was 774 tons. She was sold to L'Union des Chargeurs Coloniaux in 1897 and, although not French-built, would have qualified for some subsidy.

217

272.

273.   *LE CARBET capsized in Havre during a storm on Sept. 11th, 1903.*

218

274.

275.   *LE CARBET capsized over a Havre quay.*

276. DEANMOUNT and BOURGAINVILLE in a Bristol Channel dock.

The French barque *Bourgainville* of 1902 was one of the last of the Bounty ships to be built and was quite a smart sailer, being sunk by the U-70 off the Irish coast in 1916. The *Deanmount* was a steel full-rigger of 1791 tons, built in 1880 as the *Silvercrag*. She was named *Deanmount* when sold to R. Ferguson of Dundee in 1902. Sold to W. C. Jarvis in 1906, she was wrecked in 1910 in Aviles Bay when bound from Iquique towards Bilbao with saltpetre.

On the next page, the *Leon Blum* was a full-rigger of 2733 tons gross, also built in 1902—the last year of Bounty building. Named for one of the principal share-holders who had a ship-chandlery in San Francisco, one feels he was assured of a certain business! This ship was wrecked near Dakar in 1916.

220

277. *LEON BLUM off Hobart.*

278. ST. LOUIS and one of her sisters off Hobart.

Another of the 1902 vintage, the *St. Louis* was built by A. Dubigeon for Leon Bureau et Fils of the same port, and had a deadweight tonnage of 2700 on a nett measurement of 1779. Later she was sold to the Soc. Gen. d'Armement, and survived the war to be laid up in 1921 and scrapped in 1926. She mainly ran out to Australia and San Francisco and is here photographed off Hobart with another very typical French Bounty vessel. The split gaff topsail was very popular in these vessels and it will also be noted that she sets a small jib-headed spanker. Why her mainsail should be reefed is far from clear, but one presumes that, with her weather cloth rigged around her poop, she has just come in from sea and, possibly, hard winds to the calm of Hobart. These were very practical barques, and she has not the amount of superstructure adopted by some of her contemporaries, this being actuated by the ratio of miles sailed and gross tonnage on which the Bounty was paid. Not all ships were of the almost standard steel types spawned by the Bounty, and the old barque *Charles* is, perhaps, more typical of many that we have seen elsewhere.

279. *CHARLES of Granvelle leaving that port. Of 596 tons, she was built there in 1871. (Her royals are out of the picture.)*

280. DUCHESSE DE BERRY.

Another of the last batch of 'Bounty' ships to be built, the *Duchesse de Berry*, had a short and eventful life, appearing to be fated by the Horn. On her first voyage, after attempting to make the rounding in furious gales, she finally made San Francisco east about, after a prolonged spell in Cape Town to repair leaks: bulwarks and damage generally, and to re-stow her shifted cargo. The next voyage she again had to turn tail and run down her easting south of Australia to reach 'Frisco and, after a collision when bound to Leith, she was wrecked in the neighbourhood of Cape Horn on Penguin Rocks. Not many of the French ships of this period were painted black. She belonged to R. Guillon of Nantes, but was sold to the big Societé Genérale d'Armement of the same port before her last fatal voyage. Looking at her picture, one would hardly suppose that her gross tonnage was 2572, but her nett tonnage only 1941.

The *Ville de Mulhouse* was built in 1899 by the Chantiers de la Mediterranée for the Cie. des Voiliers Havrais, and was of 3100 tons gross, her design being based on the *President Felix Fauré* (Plate 148),

281.   VILLE DE MULHOUSE.

but she was not given that vessel's skysails, which were seldom favoured by the French. After a period in the nickel ore trade, she was sold to the Soc. Genérale d'Armement and was seen on the West coast of South America and, after the first war, spent a period running between Dakar and the River Plate, after which she was laid up in the Canal de la Martinière with so many French square-riggers. In 1927 she was sold to Chile and sailed out to Punta Arenas with a cargo of coal, after which she was hulked. However, in the Second World War, due to the shortage of tonnage, she was towed between Buenos Ayres and Punta Arenas with cargo as the *Andalucia*, after which she again reverted to her role as a hulk. When last heard of, she was sound enough and—who knows?—she may yet figure in the spate of ship restorations which is now so popular!

282. AMIRAL DE CORNULIER.

Bristol always had a great sailing ship tradition extending back to Tudor times. Many ships were built there, and the Avon saw many a tall ship coming up her stream to discharge. The *Amiral de Cornulier* is seen here lying in the port in 1921, after taking 136 days to reach the Azores for orders from Newcastle, N.S.W. She was one of the last Frenchmen to appear in Bristol, for the day of the French square-riggers was all but finished. She was laid up after discharging, and broken up in 1924. The spars of the full-rigger astern are of the *Manicia*, a Norwegian, once the lovely Whitehaven ship *Benicia*, which went over on her beam ends in the North Sea after discharging, and, after being towed into Ymuiden, was condemned. Sailing ships may not look their best in dock (though such pictures do have advantages to show various details) and it is, perhaps, more satisfying to see them as in Plate 211.

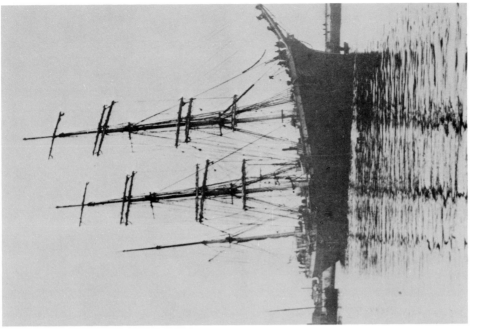

284. The GENERAL DE NEGRIER was one of the last French square-riggers left in trade, being broken up in 1928 after a disastrous voyage to Sète from the Cameroons.

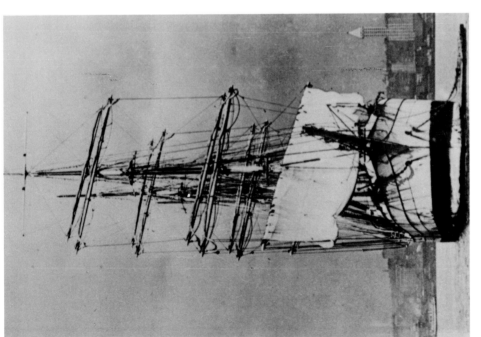

283. The French CANROBERT was sold to A. Gotaas of Christiania to become the GLITRE, under which name she is seen towing out of Seattle.

285.   L. to R.:—VERSAILLES, SØM and AREOLA.

During the great French 'Bounty' period, the Bristol Channel saw a great number of their ships. Many loaded coal outwards in South Wales for the West coast of South America and elsewhere, and many came up to the ports there to discharge. In this picture, taken in the first war, the ship on the left, the *Versailles*, is unmistakeably French with her form of painted-port side over a narrow stripe. A smart ship, she made her last passage home from Australia in 1921 and, after being laid up, was broken up in 1927.

In the centre, the *Søm* was then Norwegian and belonged to Marcussen, Jorgensen of Grimstad, having been built by Blohm and Voss for the great Hamburg Company Act. Ges, von 1896 as the *Antuco*. Later she was the *Maco* and, in 1917, was sold to S. O. Stray.*

The ship on the left was built as the *Areola T.*—a wooden barque of 923 tons—in Portland, N.B. by Hilyard Brothers in 1877. In 1900 she passed to Norway and had several Norwegian owners, but was sunk by a mine in 1917, soon after this picture was taken. The neutrality flags will be noted on the hulls of the two Norwegians.

*Of Kristianssand.

228

286. *RIVER GANGES in the Avon Gorge.*

Many the ship towing down the river from Bristol which has been snapped by a camera-man just below the Gorge. An iron barque of 642 tons, the *River Ganges* was built at Port Glasgow in 1876 for Hargrove and Hellon of Liverpool, who ran her in the East Indian and Australian trades. An older type of ship, it will be seen that she is flush-decked, and that her jib-boom is still rigged in.

Plate 287 shows H.M. Corvette *Calliope*, a composite-built 14-knot vessel, at Bristol. This ship won herself immortal fame by the seamanship exhibited in the hurricane which swept Samoa in 1889 when three American, and three German warships were lost, and when the *Calliope* alone survived of the men-o'-war present, finally steaming out between the other ships and the reef in the teeth of the wind at less than 1 knot, to make the open sea.

Plate 288 shows the French corvette *Bourgainville*, which was used as a training ship, and is often overlooked when training ships are considered. She is seen lying in St. Malo in 1904. It is interesting to compare the two vessels.

287. *H.M.S. CALLIOPE at Bristol.*

288. *Auxiliary French training barque BOURGAINVILLE.*

289.   H.M.S. ESPIEGLE.

Launched in 1880, of 1130 tons displacement, the *Espiegle* was one of fourteen composite corvettes in her class, the first seven having clipper bows and the next seven straight stems, as in this case. She was first commissioned on the Australian station and then, in 1887 (when this picture was taken), spent six years in the Pacific. On her return she was obsolete and her machinery worn out, so she was used as a boom defence vessel in Southampton.

Her picture is included simply to show that the Naval transition ships did tend to favour spencers on all masts, while there is no doubt that those more used to considering the rigging of merchant ships would find the proportions of her mizzen rigging strange. Comparisons are, of course, scarcely just, since naval vessels had a different purpose and seldom suffered from skeleton crews!

290. ST. MARY'S

Built as a U.S. Navy sloop in 1844, and kept in the Navy until 1875, when she was handed over to the New York Sea School, the *St. Mary's* saw service both in the Civil War and in Morocco. She was not a good-looking ship, appearing very bluff in her ends and with an ugly stern, but she was nevertheless very fine below the water, and became one of the best-known of all training ships. Felix Reisenberg, the well-known American sea-writer, served in her (afterwards being master in her successor, the *Newport*,) and, after she had been relegated to stationary duties for the last years of her life, Anton Otto Fischer, the great Marine Artist, spent two winters in her as an instructor. She was scrapped in 1909.

With sails beautifully stowed, her washing is a bit discordant!

291. *H.M.S. SEAFLOWER was one of the smaller brigs, 100.5 feet long and 454 tons displacement. The squadron of naval brigs, each with a complement of about 27, was one of the most successful service training schemes.*

292. H.M. brig LIBERTY.

Sister to the *Seaflower*, the *Liberty* is seen tacking. First keeping her clean full on the port tack, she was put up into the wind, whilst hauling the spanker amidships. Then, with the wind about a point on the new (starboard) bow, her mainyards are braced on to the new tack as caught by the camera in the middle of the operation, while her foreyards still box her head round. Once round, they will be braced round on to the new tack. Most of the brigs were tenders to one or other of the naval stationary training ships.

293. *H.M. brig LIBERTY entering harbour.*

294. *One of the larger brigs—either the NAUTILUS or MARTIN.*

295. *MEIJI MARU.*

The brig in Plate 294 might, superficially, appear to be the *Seaflower*, but is actually about 5 feet longer and there are minor differences. Brixham trawlers can be seen in the distance. One of the smaller brigs is coming into harbour in Plate 293. These brigs were well known around the coasts until after the turn of the century and considered to be very smartly handled by their boys. They were the last wooden ships in commission in H.M. Navy.

The vessel in Plate 295 was built in 1874 of iron as a schooner-rigged steamer for the Japanese Government by Robert Napier at Port Glasgow, but was later turned into a full-rigged training ship. She looks odd in this picture, taken in the first war with her hull dazzle-painted and the hordes of cadets on her yards. Soon afterwards she was set in a concrete berth as a stationary vessel and was certainly still there, fully-rigged, at the end of the 1939-1945 war, but was converted to a dance-hall for occupation forces! It may be thought odd that the Japanese, who had virtually no tradition of square-rig, should have operated one of the finest square-rigged school-ship schemes prior to 1942.

296. *H.M. brig SEALARK hove-to. 90 feet long, she was the smallest of the naval brigs and built in 1843.*

297. *Scene in Cardiff Docks, 1910. L. to R.:—GLUCKSTADT, MAGNA and LANGDALE.*

Merchant sailing ships did not always look their best in dock but, in fact, the loading and discharge of cargoes was their very *raison d'etre.* The ugly bald-headed full-rigger on the left is the *Gluckstadt* which was then owned by Euge. Cellier of Hamburg but which had originally been the *Glenelvan* of Sterling's 'Glen' line. (Note the absence of spanker boom and gaff.) In 1921 she became the *Landskirchen* belonging to Schröder, Hölken and Fischer, another Hamburg company but, in 1924, she was sold to Genoa and became the *Guaneri*, being abandoned in 1926 on her return voyage to Leghorn after running a cargo of marble to Rio.

The Norwegian *Magna*, at the time of the picture, was owned by P. A. Christiansen of Langesund who had bought the ship in 1892 from the Canadian Hickman fleet, for whom she had been built in Dorchester (N.B.) in 1879. After leaving Cardiff on this occasion for Walfisch Bay, she was dismasted and taken into Luderitz Bay, to be condemned.

The *Langdale* had been built in 1885 for Newton's attractive 'Dale' line but by this time was owned by R. G. Owen, who bought her in 1909.

238

298. *LIVONIA in Highbridge—a pretty brigantine built there in 1894.*

299. *One of the last sailing ships to load in Cardiff was the Chilean 5-masted barque FLORA, formerly the world-famous German POTOSI. Her cargo of coal and briquettes took fire and, abandoned with her masts gone, she went ashore on the Patagonian coast. Later she re-floated herself, and was sunk by the Argentinian cruiser PATRIA.*

300. WILLIAM at a shipyard at Pill—a very old photograph.

The trow, whose name is derived from the Anglo-Saxon word for a drinking vessel or hollow trough, was originally a double-ended open-decked barge with a single square sail working on the upper reaches of the Severn. By the 18th century there was a transom stern version and this type, though still with an open hold, trading down the lower reaches of the river and into the estuary. Between about 1840 and 1860, trows underwent more changes and were converted to ketch or sloop rig. Small dumb lighters on the Avon, which were similar to trows, retained the square sail for use in favourable winds. Trows survived into the 20th century, mainly in the Forest of Dean coal trade, and a few remained under sail until the 1930's.

301. Trow *PRUDENCE, built at Salop in 1822.*

302. Trow *JONADAB, built in 1845, re-built in 1895, was of 68 tons and owned by Wm. James, of Saul, Gloucester.*

303. 3-masted schooner ELLEN, ex FRITZ, off the Mersey.

All manner of vessels visited the Mersey. This trim schooner of 305 tons was built in Martenshoek in 1914 but, when the picture was taken, was owned in Marstal, Denmark. She was lost in 1928.

Liverpool, like all ports, had its quota of smaller craft, and Plate 304 shows the Canning Dock in 1885 with the ketch *Windward* in the centre. The large domed building in the background is the Customs House, Canning Place, erected on the site of the first dock which closed in 1826. It was badly damaged in the Second World War and subsequently demolished. A tower block of offices and factories now stands on the site. In 1892-3 the Liverpool overhead railway was built and opened, and would have shown in the picture in which an old horse bus can be seen clearly, together with two cutters (collectively known locally as 'smacks') trading between Liverpool and the small Welsh ports, such as Caernarvon. They often carried the fair weather square sails which can be seen. The probability is that the nearest one came from Wales, due to the stone cargo piled up on the quayside, since this was a common enough freight for them.

304. *Liverpool Customs House and Canning Dock in 1895.*

305. CHRISTEL VINNEN, ex CALIFORNIA, making her last passage.

Liverpool Docks were a forest of masts and spars at the turn of the century. By common consent, the White Star 4-masted barque *California* was one of the finest owned in the port. John Masefield did her scant justice in describing her as "huge, as slow as time" when finding a word to rhyme with 'sublime'! After spending a year under Ritson and Livesey of the same port, she became the *Alster*, owned by Sloman's of Hamburg and then she passed to Schramm's of Bremen as the *Christel Vinnen*. Interned in Valparaiso in 1914, she was damaged by her crew and then hulked but was re-rigged in 1926 in the midst of the depression and sent through Panama to Norfolk (Va), being wrecked on Old Providence Island *en voyage*. Law's *Elginshire*, of Glasgow, survived to be one of the last British 4-masted barques, making her last passage in 1921, while Macvicar, Marshall's *Forteviot*, seen with her mizzen topgallant-mast sent down, became the *Werner Vinnen*, but was taken as a prize in the first war to be re-named first *Yawry* and then, under J. J. Bell of Hull, *Bellands*, under both British and Norwegian registry. She was broken up in 1925. *Westland* was a famous Shaw, Savill New Zealand trader.

306. *The Queen's Dock, Liverpool on May 16th, 1895. Barque INCA on left, with the CALIFORNIA left centre. Right foreground is s.s. LOANDA with flats alongside. Ahead of her lie the FORTEVIOT, WESTLAND and ELGINSHIRE. The identity of the distant ships is not known.*

The Flats were the sailing barges of the Mersey and its tributary river, the Weaver. As the name suggests, they were flat-bottomed, with a rounded bilge and a neat but short entry and run aft. Their hull timbers were massive; the keelson and hog piece* often being as much as three feet deep. They were steered by a huge rudder hung outboard on the sternpost. Both transom and pointed stern flats were built, but the transom stern seems to be the older type. Flats changed from a single square-sail to sloop rig in the eighteenth century. Like the Thames barge, they traded outside their own estuary and along the adjacent coastline to North Wales and the Lancashire ports. Their sailing gear was very heavy. For example, the mainsail boom could measure as much as fifty feet in length and fourteen inches in diameter. Their standing rigging was wire rope except for the forestay, which was a wrought iron rod. Their sails (mainsail and foresail) were tanned a splendid red with red ochre and fish oil. The mainsail was cut with a characteristically high peak. Flats were usually worked by a crew of two or three if working coastwise, and there were winches at the foot of the mast to enable them to work the halliards. Flatmen were very knowledgeable about the tides and the mud flats of the river, manoeuvring their bulky craft in and out of dock with breathtaking ease.

As flats increased in size in the latter part of the nineteenth century, a number of ketch-rigged or 'jigger' flats were launched. Most of the jigger flats worked in the coasting trade and some were fitted with auxiliary engines in the 1920's. Very few flats remained under sail by that time. They mainly traded out of Widnes West Dock with sand and chemicals. Many others remained afloat, but reduced to dumb barges. The last flat to work under sail in the Mersey was probably the *Keskadale*, which continued in the sand business until the mid-1940's. No sailing flat has been preserved, but a number of hulks survive and the dumb flat *Mossdale*, which has the same lines as a sailing flat, has been preserved at the North-Western Canal Boat Museum, in Ellesmere Port, and there are models of sailing flats in the Merseyside County Museum at Liverpool. Flats may also be seen in Plates 306, 307 and 309, and, like the other forms of local craft, their passing must be cause for regret.

*A timber running fore-and-aft, bolted to the top of the keel, providing a landing edge for the garboard strakes.

307. *Mersey Flats.*

308. MOUNT STEWART towing down to the Tuskar Rock.

Built in 1891, the *Mount Stewart* was one of the last two square-riggers built specifically for the wool trade. She was broken up in 1924 after discharging a cargo of nitrate from Chile.

Originally full-rigged, the *Valparaiso*, of 730 tons, was built in Liverpool for Balfour's and was bigger than most of the flush-decked copper-ore fleet which were said to have the hardest trade in the world. The manner of stowing her gaff topsail is worth noting. The copper-oremen, mainly associated with Swansea, were the commercial pioneers of the Horn with double topgallant backstays always rigged, running coal out to Chile and ore home, stowed in a trunk. Their main keelsons were four feet high and they had two bilge keelsons of similar height, the trunk being above them and narrowing as it rose, to preserve a proper stability with so heavy a cargo.

248

309. *VALPARAISO, one of the famous copper-ore-men.*

310. ANDRADA in Liverpool.

With her cargo almost discharged, the *Andrada*, built in 1891 by Pickersgill's for Roberts, was of 2593 tons and completed shortly before their more famous *Andhorina* which, as the *Helène*, became the biggest of A. D. Bordes' nitrate fleet and, like the *Muskoka* (as the *Caroline*) retained her skysails under the French who, although seldom building skysail-yarders, usually retained them in bought ships. The *Andrada* went missing in 1900.

In this age of container and roll-on, roll-off ships, and of gangs of derricks, it is worth noting the single gin block through which a whip is rove above each of her three hatches. This was the normal mode of discharging which was, needless to say, extremely slow.

The *Allonby*, owned by Leyland's of Liverpool, was a barque of 1400 tons built in 1882, and is here seen making sail after casting off her tug near the Tuskar Light.

311. ALLONBY making sail near the Tuskar Rock.

312. SCOTTISH LOCHS in tow.

Built in Southampton in 1888, the *Scottish Lochs* was one of W. H. Ross and Co.'s smart 'Scottish' line. Later sold to G. Windrum of Liverpool with the rest of the fleet, she passed to that great Norwegian owner S. O. Stray in 1912, being renamed *Søfareren* (Seafarer) and was only broken up in 1928. She had called in to Queenstown prior to the taking of Plate 312 to receive her orders for discharging port. Since economics were not pressing quite so harshly on the sailing ship in those days, she is being towed to Liverpool. Having a fair wind, she has set five topsails to aid the tug. The courses were seldom set on such occasions, in order to leave the helmsman a clear view.

In the last days of deep-water merchant sail, when the margin between profit and loss was so small, towage was kept to a bare minimum but, until the outbreak of the first war, it was no uncommon thing for a vessel to be towed—say—from Hamburg to Liverpool, or vice versa, the sailing ship often being manned by a crowd of runners, who were not properly her crew, but signed on for the 'run' between ports.

313. *PARTHENOPE, seen in a Liverpool dry-dock, was built by Evans of that port in 1875 for J. Heap's and had a successful career as a wool clipper. In 1897 she was sold to D. Olivari of Genoa and re-named PELLEGRINA O. She went missing between Newcastle, N.S.W. and Antofagasta in 1907. (The Italians bought a number of beautiful clippers.)*

314. CITY OF ADELAIDE, in New Zealand waters.

Apart from the Down-Easter *Olympic*, the only other 4-masted sailing vessels rigged with square-yards on fore and main and fore-and-aft on the main and mizzen were the *Omeo* (built Newcastle 1858) and the *City of Adelaide* seen above, built in Glasgow in 1864 and registered in Sydney. A more elusive vessel was the *Mersey*, of London, built there in 1859. All these three were converted steamers. The *Olympic* later became a barquentine. The *City of Adelaide* must not be confused with the clipper of that name, now doing duty as H.M.S. *Carrick* in the Clyde.

More steamers were converted to sail (and *vice versa*) than is generally supposed. At the end of the first war, some uncompleted Ferris-type steamers in the United States were finished as 5-masted barquentines. One such was the *Anne Comyn*, of 2265 gross tons, which is seen here behind a swell off the Mersey Bar on her maiden voyage. The swell flatters her by concealing her ugly straight stem. Her sisters were the *Phyllis Comyn, Katherine Mackall*, and *Haviside*, none of which lasted long, though this was mainly due to the slump.

254

315. *ANNE COMYN behind the swell off the Bar light ship.*

316. The LANCING, one of the most famous of the conversions from steam to sail, was originally the PEREIRE, a fast transatlantic passenger steamer.

317. *The largest and, arguably, the ugliest sailing ship ever built and the only 7-masted schooner, was the steel THOMAS W. LAWSON of 5218 tons. Launched in 1902 for the Chesapeake Bay coal trade, she was not wholly successful; spent a lot of her time at sea under tow, and was finally wrecked and smashed on the Scillies in wild weather.*

318. NAVAHOE and IROQUOIS.

The Anglo-American Oil Co. had a fine fleet of square-rigged oil carrying sailing ships but, in 1908, built the *Navahoe*, rigged as a 6-masted bald-headed schooner. Since she was not manoeuvreable on her own, she cannot be classed as a sailing vessel, although it is true that she did carry her big lowers in the wildest weather. Her purpose was to carry oil in bulk across the Atlantic—mainly to the Thames, and she was towed by the *Iroquois*, a 10,000-ton tanker equipped with special heavy-duty towing gear. The *Navahoe*'s sails were hoisted by steam and in Plate 318 the 'Horse and Cart', as they were termed, are about to start a transatlantic tow.

The Americans, above all nations, built big schooners. The really big ones, used on the East coast coal trade, were not really successful, since there were limits to the useful size of the rig and they had disadvantages on deep-sea voyages. Perhaps the most successful ones were owned on the West coast, in the Pacific trade.

The *Honolulu*, (Plate 319) of 1060 tons gross was built in 1896 by R. Dawson for Johnson of Honolulu while Plate 321 shows the *William Nottingham*, of 1204 tons and built in 1902 at Ballard, to trade successfully for a number of years for the Globe Navigation Co. until relegated to a barge. The vast number of wooden sailing ships built around Puget Sound is not generally appreciated.

319.   *4-masted schooner HONOLULU.*

320. KINEO arriving at Galveston, Texas.

The *Kineo* was the last vessel built by Sewall's of Bath and was built of steel. Apart from the *Thos. W. Lawson* and the 6-master *William L. Douglas*, she was the only big American steel-built schooner. They had toyed with the idea of a 5-masted barquentine, but finally launched the *Kineo* in 1903. They had reckoned her to carry some 3500 tons coasting and 3000 when deep-sea, but she made one epic voyage in 1905-06 from Norfolk (Va.) to Manila: on to Brisbane, Newcastle, Kahului and home to Philadelphia and, although she did well in the Trades, the wear and tear on her gear: her gaffs, mast-hoops and sails was unbelievable. She had to reduce sail both in very heavy and in light weather, and never made another deep-sea voyage of this sort. As previously stated, the apparent economic advantages of the schooner rig are not borne out in practice on long voyages, although they have proved excellent on specific runs or coastwise.

Finally, in 1916, she was sold to The Texas Co. and she became converted into the motor-ship *Maryland*. Whether Sewall's would have repeated the experiment had they continued to build is doubtful.

321. *WILLIAM NOTTINGHAM with a deck-load of lumber.*

322. TITANIA.

Sad to relate, most vessels built with unusual or freak rigs have been actuated by considerations of economy rather than efficiency. These considerations were seldom realised. Capt. Fairlie thought in 1893 that the square-rigger was ceasing to be an economic proposition and designed rather unusual 4-masted barquentines with a square yard on main and mizzen—or on mizzen and jigger. The *Oberon* and *Titania* were built for his own account. The picture above is of poor quality, but shows her sail plan. The *Renfield* was built for S. A. Russell, *Sound of Jura* for Chas. Walker and the *Westfield* for Nicholl of Dundee. Of 1119 gross, 1054 nett and 1740 deadweight tonnage, they had a 500-ton water ballast tank amidships, which was not usual at that time, and had standing gaffs with brailing lowers. These vessels were by no means failures, though the experiment was not repeated. Undoubtedly the brailing sails had advantages over hoisting sails, since the hoops had a relatively short life in deep-sea voyages, due to wear and tear.*

*See page 260.

323. *Barquentine WESTFIELD, flying the Blue Peter, prepares for sea. Passing to Italy in 1921 to be re-named FELICE, she was wrecked two years later.*

324. A fine quartering wind.

Reminiscent of Briscoe's 'The Dreamer', the carpenter of the *Pommern* meditates as the ship churns on with a fine quartering wind—the whole atmosphere so different from a ship in dock. Built on the Clyde in 1904 by J. Reid for B. Wencke Sohne of Hamburg as the *Mneme*, she was bought by Laeisz's Flying 'P' line in 1907 and, after being laid up when handed to the allies as war reparations in 1919, she finally came under the house-flag of Gustaf Erikson of Mariehamn, where she is still preserved.

Capt. Fairlie's *Oberon*, sister to the *Titania* and *Westfield*, passed to J. M. Larsen of Odense in Denmark, who had several square-riggers. At some point her rig was altered to a conventional bald-headed barquentine, as she is seen in the picture opposite when lying in Hamburg, light ship. When this change occurred is not clear, but it certainly did not improve her appearance although she retains her name—Oberon—King of the Fairies!

325. *OBERON, with altered rig, lies in Hamburg.*

326.   Abandoning the dismasted PINNAS, ex FITZJAMES.

That a large proportion of the finest sailing ships ever known were built on the Clyde would not be denied by any Clydesider and is attested by the many foreign buyers who bought the ships or who placed orders in the yards. The *Eva Montgomery* was not launched until 1901, when the clipper ship was long past, but she and her sisters were reckoned to be the fastest all-round ships of this century. Built for Montgomery's of London (whose house-flag she flies), she passed to the Act. Ges. von 1896 of Hamburg in 1909 and went missing as the *Orla* in 1912. One of her sisters was the *Ladye Doris*, which became the *Oliva*, in the same company while the other, the *Fitzjames*, was bought by the Laeisz Flying 'P' line of Hamburg to become the *Pinnas* and maintain that company's high traditions until she was off the Horn in April, 1929. Beset by furious gales, the wind suddenly dropped and left her rolling to a degree that her masts came down, smashing the main pumps. Her rudder was gone, she was leaking and, although she had radioed for help, this was delayed owing to renewed hurricane force winds.

266

327. *EVA MONTGOMERY — a ship famed for her chanteying.*

328. GRACE HARWAR and POMMERN in the lower reaches of the Thames.

The first of Montgomery's steel ships was the *Grace Harwar* which proved to be the last European full-rigged ship in trade. She had a chequered career, both under the British and Finnish flags, and was finally broken up in 1935 after making her best passage back from Australia in years—98 days from Port Broughton to Falmouth.

All these Montgomery ships mentioned were built by Wm. Hamilton, and, only four years later, he built one of his last in the form of the huge 4-masted barque *Kurt*, for William Siemers of Hamburg. Superficially similar to the later German-built 'P' 4-masters, she had a shorter poop and one or two minor differences. Some say she was the finest square-rigger built in the twentieth century and, latterly, as the American and, later, Finnish *Moshulu* (being Gustaf Erikson's last deep-sea acquisition) she was certainly the largest sailing vessel afloat and in commission. No ship looks her best light and from the weather quarter, especially when she has a Liverpool section, but Plate 329 shows her setting sail in these conditions with the upper spanker being set. Double spankers may have been ugly, but they were immensely practical. Since the last war, this wretched ship has been hawked about as a hulk and is now destined to become some sort of floating restaurant since the South Street Museum in New York decided not to restore her.

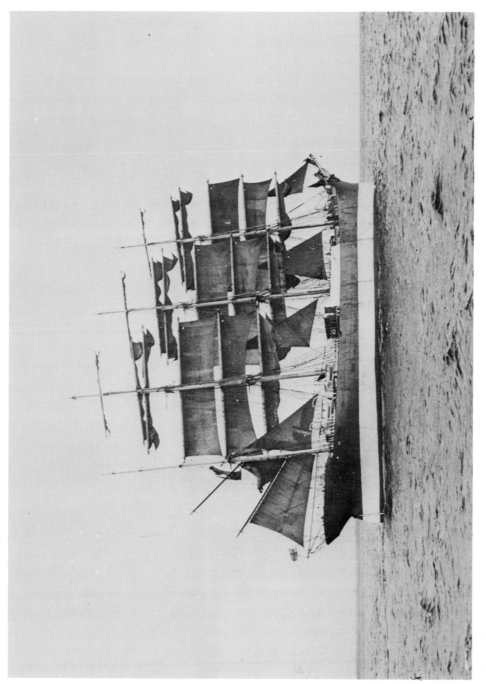

329. The *MOSHULU, ex DREADNOUGHT, ex KURT was an immensely strong and powerful vessel. She is here making a departure.*

330. JASON.

Although the prime purpose of a merchant ship was to carry remunerative freights, some owners *did* pay a good deal of attention to both fittings and appearance in the Golden Age of Sail, and it is commonly said that Carmichael's Golden Fleece line were perhaps the best looking of all, taken as a fleet. Certainly the proportions of their spar plans left nothing to be desired aesthetically, and their performances were in the first class. Built by Barclay, Curle in 1870, after their *Golden Fleece*, the *Jason* was 1512 tons and one of the best examples of the company.

The *Peleus*, last of their full-riggers and built in 1892, was not so attractive, the jibboom having given way to a spike bowsprit: the main skysail had disappeared, and there was a bridge abaft her mainmast with a flying bridge fore-and-aft. The bridge was not a solid section, as in later 4-masters. Extremely functional, she was bought by A. D. Bordes and re-named *Adolphe* to replace their 4-masted barque of that name after her loss. (See page 116.)

331.   *PELEUS, later ADOLPHE, scrapped in Holland in 1923.*

332. INVERTROSSACHS in the Clyde.

When a ship was brand new her sails would be supplied by a sail-making loft who were responsible for bending them. Very often the jibs and staysails were simply bent on to the halliards in their stops and so hoisted, as in this case. (And see Plate 333.) Very occasionally a master would revert to this system in port, believing it to be the acme of smartness, but not everybody would agree on the excellence of the effect so attained. Since the sheets were not shackled on to the clews, they could not be broken out instantly as in modern yachting practice.

This vessel is the 4-masted barque *Invertrossachs*, one of so many which seem to have been overlooked by historians. She was built in 1891 by Russell's for David Bruce's Dundee clipper line, of 2710 gross tons, and was sent out to Philadelphia to load case oil, but never arrived, being posted as missing in February 1892. Few ships had a shorter life.

272

333. The WILLSCOTT, of 2615 tons, was another vessel built by Wm. Hamilton for Hickie, Borman, but was sold to San Francisco two years later in 1898, passing to the Alaska packers salmon cannery operation in 1908 as the STAR OF ICELAND, and being broken up in Japan in 1929.

334. VANDUARA.

Taking her name, like most of J. D. Clink's fleet, from a famous racing yacht, the *Vanduara* was very fast. This is more than can be said for the later vessels in the company. It is a pity that her main and mizzen skysail yards are not crossed in this picture of her as originally rigged while she lay off Greenock, as she was a fine-looking and speedy ship. Later she was stripped of her jigger yards and converted to a 4-masted barque, being sunk by enemy action in 1917. Built in 1887, she was just over 2000 registered tons and this is interesting, since the general effect of the 4-masted full-riggers which, with a few exceptions, were not unduly large, was always to make them appear to be much bigger than was actually the case.

As has been pointed out elsewhere in this book, the jigger yards of a 4-master (or mizzen yards of a 3-master) were of very doubtful value, tending to make the ship gripe with the wind forward of the beam, and throwing her about with the wind aft. On balance, they probably did more harm than good.

335.   The *LADY WENTWORTH* was built in 1896 for Adam Hamilton of Greenock, but passed to H. Fölsch of Hamburg to be the *WÖGLINDE* in 1905.   Here she has a tug fore and aft as she leaves the yard of Scott & Co, her builders.   She was broken up in 1930.

336. LAURA, hove-to.

If a sailing ship wished to take off her way—to 'stop', in common terms—she needed to so manoeuvre that some of her sails were acting in opposition to the others. If a ship was running free, the helm was put up and the fore-yards run forward, as in Plate 338. A sailing ship's masts are really a series of levers and, although it might seem that two masts drawing one way and one the other would not stop the ship, one must take into account the trim of the ship, since she is usually loaded somewhat by the stern. If she is reaching the mainyards are squared. In the case of the *Laura* the head-yards are aback, but the main and mizzen sails drawing. Any adjustment can be made by clewing up one or another sail, as in the case of the *Antares*, (Plate 342). Originally the British *Sutlej*, built in 1888, she was at this time owned by Semidei Bros. of Genoa and went missing between Marseilles and Sydney in 1914.

276

338. *Andrew Weir's OLIVEBANK hove-to for her pilot in the Clyde.*

337. *MOSHULU hove-to to tranship an injured man. The port boat is in the water. Boats were not always launched as fast as one would like to think—sometimes being painted in to their chocks!*

339. OLIVEBANK in Spencer Gulf on her last deep-water voyage, 1939.

Andrew Weir's 'Bank' line were large and powerful carriers, built in an era of falling freight rates when speed was no longer the prime criterion. When the company sold their sailing ships, several were quickly snapped up by the Norwegians, the *Olivebank* becoming the *Caledonia*, but her original name was restored when she was later purchased by Capt. Gustaf Erikson of Mariehamn. In Plate 339 she has just left Port Victoria with a cargo of wheat. Having discharged in Barry, she was bound for her home port when the war broke out and hit a mine off the Danish coast, sinking quickly with some loss of life.

The picture of the *Springbank*, built in Port Glasgow in 1894, two years after the *Olivebank*, may be unfortunate, but it does show the inherent power of the ship and, at the same time, the ugliness of the 'bald-headed' rig (double topgallantsails with no royals above them). She became the Norwegian *Asrym*. Aesthetically, single topgallants and royals was the most pleasing combination, and if the ship carried skysails, she often looked better still. Yet even the sails of a 'bald-header', caught by the rising sun, (Plate 340) as seen by the helmsman, had a certain fascination.

278

341. *SPRINGBANK – a very square bald-header.*

340. *POMMERN's mizzen yards at sunrise.*

342. *ANTARES, ex SUTLEJ, hove-to.*

The *Antares* was an iron ship built by Russell's on the Clyde for Foley & Co. of London, and was mainly trading East until sold to the Italians. Launched in 1888, she was 1742 tons.

The *Zippora* is seen making her departure from the Clyde. A wooden barque built in Haugesund in 1878, she was owned by two Norwegian firms before being sold to Sweden, and was still afloat in 1925, being 890 tons. A man is seen aloft ready to overhaul the royal buntlines as the sail is hoisted. (It will be noted that she has no topsail buntlines.) The catfall tackle is overhauled and, shortly, a man will be sent down in a bowline to hook it on to the ring on the anchor shank prior to catting it and securing it inboard for her voyage.

Siedenbrug, Wendt & Co. of Bremen had bought in a number of wooden American-built ships, of which the *George* was one. Originally built in Boston as the *Star of Hope* in 1869 (1195 tons nett) she became the Dutch *Ster der Hoop* before assuming German registry.

344. *The Bremen ship GEORGE's appearance bespeaks her Down-East origins.*

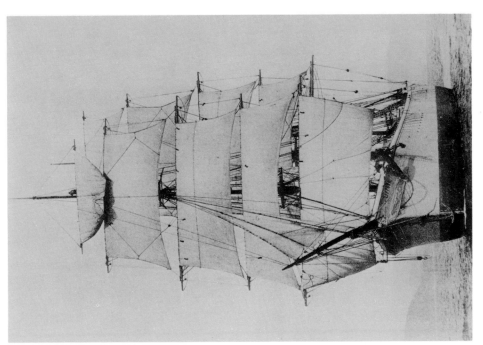

343. *ZIPPORA.*

345. *SOPHIE.*

Hit by a steamer just above her counter, the damage was never likely to be mortal, but it does give an idea of the force of the impact. It is interesting to set a glass against the picture to enlarge the ends of the planking on the poop.

The vessel is the full-rigger *Sophie*, built in 1883 as the *Sierra Lucena*—one of the lovely all-white Sierra line. Then she became the *Inveruglas*, but was sold to Norway in 1907 when she was named *Sophie*, bearing this name for a short period during the First World War, rather curiously, under the Swiss flag. Finally, as the *Tusitala* (Teller of Tales), named for Robert Louis Stevenson, she had the distinction of being the last American square-rigger in trade—apart from a few Second World War temporary resuscitations. Latterly, she was running between New York and Honolulu, making the passage through the Panama Canal.

346. *Built by Russell & Co, who built so **many** square-riggers, for W. O. Taylor's 'Glen' line of Dundee in 1899, the GLENMARK was 1257 tons nett. She is evidently about to get under weigh, since her foc's'le head rail is removed and the catfall overhauled ready to take the anchor when it is raised.*

347. Isle of Man nickie HONEY GUIDE in Baltasound, Shetland, 1900.

From St. Ives in Cornwall to Baltasound, the most northerly haven in Shetland, is a long sail, and one might well be surprised to encounter there a lugger of such obviously Cornish descent as the Manx nickie *Honey Guide*, CT 96, of Casletown, Plate 347, photographed under sail there in the year 1900. The explanation must be sought in the mid-eighteen-sixties, when the Manx fishermen became aware of the superiority in speed and weatherliness of the Cornish luggers from St. Ives then coming to the island and using its ports as bases from which to fish mackerel and herring in the Irish Sea. Because so many of the Cornishmen bore the name Nicholas, their boats were commonly referred to as the 'Nickies', and when craft of similar construction and rig came to be built in the Isle of Man, from about 1869 onwards, the name stuck and they were known as Manx nickies ever after.

Like most drift net fishing boats, they followed the shoals as they moved round the coasts, and that is how the *Honey Guide* came to Baltasound. Great was the variety of craft to be found in Shetland waters in those days and a photograph, Plate 348, taken at Lerwick

348. *Old sailing types in Lerwick harbour, c. 1895.*

about 1895, shows four distinct types under way in the harbour. These are, in order of sailing:— The Isle of Man nickie *Full Moon*, of Peel; the Shetland herring cutter *Rosebank*, of Sandwick; the scaffie *Elsie Main*, of Portnockie, and, following up astern, a coasting ketch. Of all the places in the British Isles, Shetland has retained more of the Viking influence in the model of its local craft than is apparent anywhere else, and this is most strongly evident in the delightful 1904 photograph, Plate 349, of Whalsey fourerns becalmed. These double-ended clinker-built craft, with their graceful sheer and very square-headed dipping lug sails, so close in rig to the original pattern of the longships, with their single square sail on a single mast stepped nearly amidships, are themselves but smaller versions of the larger sixerns, or six-oared boats, in which the Shetland haaf, or deep-sea fishing, was carried on until towards the end of the nineteenth century. Even the sail in a fourern was called a 'swares'l'—never a lug. It was the great gale of 20th July, 1881, when 10 boats and 58 men were lost, that spelt the final blow to the open 6-oared craft.

285

349. *Whalsey fourerns becalmed, 1904.*

Although the Viking influence remained strongest in Shetland, which retained its close relationship with Norway through the centuries, it left a marked heritage in the shape of local types of craft that have been developed to suit local conditions on all the shores along which the longships plied. This was particularly true in Scotland, where the oldest of the three main types of fishing boats were the scaffies, similar to the *Elsie Main* in Plate 348. These were distinguished by their clinker build and their very steeply-sloping stem and stern-posts. Rigged with a dipping lug foresail and a standing lug mizzen, their short keel made them quick in stays; but their full bow sections made them slow to windward, when they pounded badly.

Next to be mentioned are the fifies, which had almost vertical stem and stern-posts, the later craft being carvel-built. In rig, they were much like the scaffies, but being longer on the keel and with a deep forefoot, they were faster to windward, but slow in stays. Then,

286

351. *Inverness zulus putting to sea. The nearer is a big one.*

350. *Inverness fifie—IN 49.*

352. Fraserburgh zulus in a fresh breeze.

in 1879, William Campbell of Lossiemouth combined the straight vertical stem of the fifie with the raking stern-post of the scaffie in a craft named the *Nonesuch*. It has been said that this was done to settle a dispute between a fisherman and his wife who were to be the joint owners of the new boat, one wanting a scaffie and the other a fifie! Whether that be true or not, the new type was an immediate success, and many more were built thereafter.

Because they were introduced at the time of the Zulu War, they acquired the generic term of 'zulus', and they were among the last to survive of the old Scottish fishing craft from the days of sail. They became common on the east coasts from the Moray Firth to Shetland, and in the Hebrides, particularly in Stornoway in the west, where the

353. Zulus at sea. Note timber-heads disclosed by absence of covering boards.

last six zulus still fishing under sail alone continued to do so until after the First World War. Some very big zulus were built, up to 84 ft. in overall length, and in such craft the enormous fore lug, rising to a height of some 70 ft. on a mast without stays or shrouds and supported only by the halyard on the weather side, must have been an extremely powerful sail.

The photographs will give a good idea of the appearance of the smaller zulus under sail as seen from many angles. It is noteworthy, however, that in none of them, almost without exception, is the mizzen set. One inevitably wonders why? It is interesting, too, to observe the yard in the nearest zulu in Plate 352, since it is clearly feeling the weight of the wind.

354. Barque NESCIO at Kragero.

Once the slump had set in after the first war, it was only rarely that a sailing vessel could arrive in a port and find more than one or two of her own kind but, previously, especially twenty years earlier, every port of almost any degree would have its quota at all times, whether big or small. Very attractive they looked in the older world towns, when several vessels would be drying off their sails at once. The *Nescio* was actually built in Kragero in 1870 and was a small barque of only 278 tons.

In the dock scene opposite, the full-rigger on the right is the *Buenos Ayres*, ex *Hilbre* ex *William Law*: the little painted-port iron barque is the *Hudson*, which long ran to New Zealand for Shaw Savill's before being sold to France. Ahead lie Andrew Weir's *Thistlebank* alongside the French Bounty ship *Maréchal de Castries*. The identity of the other vessels has not been ascertained. There are ten square-riggers visible in the picture, and this was little enough. The contrast between the *Hudson*—a big ship in her day—and the barque alongside her, built two or three decades later, is interesting.

290

355. *Dock scene at the turn of the century.* (*See opposite page.*)

356. *Launch of the ELLERBANK at Maryport in 1885.*

Constricted water demanded a broadside launch and, with such a vessel as the *Ellerbank*, of 1426 tons nett, a large crowd was attracted to watch the scene. Most would have some knowledge of ships. She was built by Roberts for McDiarmid, Greenshields & Co.

Plate 357 was taken about 1910 in the Little Mystic Dock at Boston, Mass, and shows the sailing fleet loading lumber for the River Plate. The *Gael* was a steel barque of 1630 tons gross, built in 1893 by Russell's of Port Glasgow for D. McGillivray of Greenock:* Astern is the *Mincio*, built as Fernie's *Cleomene*, an iron ship of 1797 tons built by T. R. Oswald of Southampton in 1877 but sold to the Soc. R. Gualino of Genoa in 1908 and scrapped in 1924. Inside her is one of the most interesting square-riggers of all time, for the *Pass of Balmaha*, taken over by the Germans in 1914, became the historic sailing raider *See-Adler*, under the no less famous Count Graf von Luckner, to sink many sailing ships in an epic cruise of adventure and honour, which ended when she was lost in a typhoon on Mopelia Island. The *Timandra* was built by Duncan's for H. J. Olive.

*Not to be confused with the French barque *Gaël*, which was abandoned the previous year.

357. The lumber fleet loading at Little Mystic Dock, Boston, Mass. about 1910. In the foreground the barque GAEL lies outside the 1112-ton barque SNOWDEN, built by Russell's in 1877. Astern of them is the TIMANDRA, of 1579 tons built in 1885, outside the Glasgow ship PASS OF BALMAHA, built in 1888 by Duncan's for the River Plate Shipping Co. Of 1571 tons, she later became the notorious SEE-ADLER. Astern of the TIMANDRA is the Italian MINCIO, ex CLEOMENE. In the rear are two American schooners.

358. INVERCAULD running down her Easting.

The run between Australia and the Horn, or from the South Atlantic to Australia, involved a long run East through the high latitudes, usually with a fair wind and often with hard weather. The *Invercauld*, with mainsail fast, is getting along well, and was one of a series of barques of 1400-1500 tons owned by Geo. Milne's Inver line. Sold out of the company in 1916, she was torpedoed soon afterwards.

Port Augusta is right at the head of Spencer Gulf. The *Oakland* was a small wooden barque of 484 tons nett, built in 1865 in Bath, Me. for W. P. Sayward of Port Madison, and later owned in Seattle by A. O. Nelson while the *Peri*, built in 1868 by Softley of S. Shields of iron was later cut down to a barque and lengthened from 195 to 212 feet, which accounts for her hogged appearance. At this time she belonged to John Stewarts, who bought her from W. Wright of S. Shields. Sold to Norway in 1906, she was broken up in 1910.

294

359. Port Augusta in 1886. L. to R.:— PERI, THUNDERBOLT, DURISDEER and OAKLAND. The THUNDERBOLT, of 1193 tons, was built in 1863 by Samuelson's of Hull for Burgess of London. The DURISDEER had been built in 1864 by Stephen's for Smith's famous 'City' line as the CITY OF LAHORE, but was owned by T. C. Guthrie of Glasgow in 1886.

360. KAISER, alongside in Hobart.

Hobart was a port of call for sailing ships of all nationalities, and here we see the wooden German *Kaiser*, built in 1877 by H. F. Ulrichs of Bremerhaven for the well-known German firm, D. H. Watjen & Co, being 1280 tons nett. There is the bow of a Bordes 4-master just visible on the left of the picture. The French ships became the most common visitors to the port, since the workings of their Bounty system, revolving around gross tonnage and miles sailed, favoured calls at such far-off ports! The *Kaiser* was laid up in the Geestemunde Canal in 1920 and was then sold to W. Schluchmann of Geestemunde in the following year, and by that time was probably the last surviving wooden deep-sea German sailing ship.

Plate 361 shows the legendary Circular Quay at Sydney with, nearest the camera, the *Candida*, one of nine fast and beautiful sisters built at Whitehaven to load some 1800 tons. She, with the *Greta* and *Angerona*, belonged to Lowden, Edgar & Co. Circular Quay, alas, is no longer circular, but a series of ferry terminals.

361. *CANDIDA, loading at Circular Quay, Sydney.*

362. *MERMERUS, one of the most beautiful of Carmichael's wool clippers, loading at Williamstown. Sold to Mariehamn in 1909, she was the fastest ship owned in the Åland Islands, being wrecked near Christianssand in 1909.*

363. DARTFORD, resuscitated from being a hulk.

Built as a full-rigged ship of 1327 tons by Iliffe & Mounsey of Sunderland in 1877 for J. T. North of London, the *Dartford* passed successively to G. Traill & Co. and W. H. Corsar's 'Flying Horse' line and then to the Union S.S. Co. of New Zealand in 1908. She then became a sail-training vessel for the company, carrying cargo and cadets, mainly in the trans-Pacific trade, with great success. After four years she was hulked but, due to the shipping shortage in the first war, was re-rigged as a barque, as she appears in Plate 363, and was given two more years of active life before reverting to a hulk which was finally broken up in 1946.

There were some fine little barques and barquentines in the Tasman Sea trade, one of which was the *Rothesay Bay*, an iron barque built in 1877 at Dumbarton, which passed to Norway for a time as the *Activ*.

365.

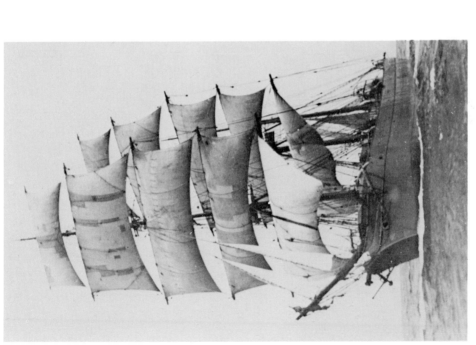

364.

ROTHESAY BAY, ex ACTIV, ex ROTHESAY BAY.

366. SENATOR VERSMANN at Port Adelaide.

There has been so much written of the Laeisz 'P' line, Wencke's, Rickmers, Vinnens, and other great German companies, that it is easy to forget the enormous scope of that country's sailing operations, and the fact that their ships might be found all over the world.

The *Senator Versmann* was built at Rostock in 1889 for A. H. Wappäus of Hamburg but, in 1904, was sold to J. Wimmer of the same port and re-named *Sachsen* and, in the following year, experienced one of the most extraordinary mirages ever known.* In 1915 she became the Portuguese *Portugal*, being by then barque-rigged.

Built in 1921 (hardly a propitious time to build) by Krupps for F. A. Vinnen, at the same time as some strange 5-masted auxiliary freak-rigged schooners, the *Magdalene Vinnen* was given an auxiliary and steel well-decks. Whether her engine compensated for the lost freight is doubtful. Her midship section was exceptionally long and, in 1936, she became the Nord Deutscher Lloyd training ship *Kommodore Johnsen*, but was taken over by Russia after the war as the sail-training ship *Sedov*.

*See Square-Riggers, The Final Epoch, 1921-1958, page 454.

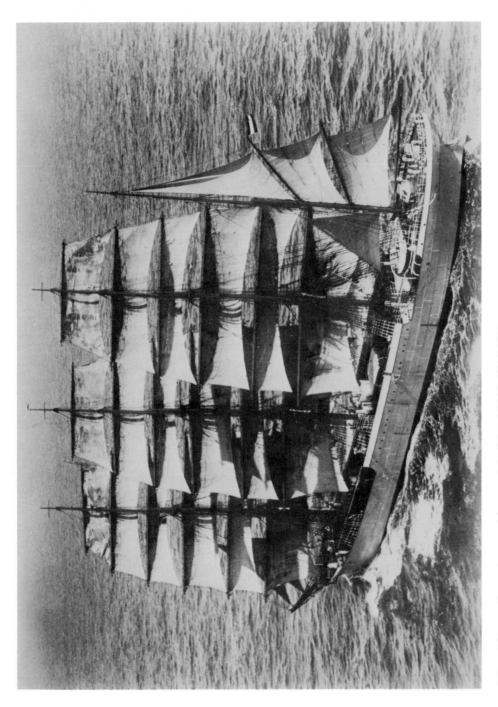

367. *The auxiliary 4-masted barque MAGDALENE VINNEN.*

368. PHOS, lying off Hobart.

Said to be heavy to work by those who sailed in her, the Norwegian *Phos*, built in 1893 of 1893 tons at Rostock for Eugene Collet of Christiania achieved a good deal of publicity on the Australian coast in 1897 when the Customs authorities found secret lockers beautifully constructed (by the ship's carpenter) in the saloon and chart-houses, which were being used for smuggling. Stories circulated—as stories will—that the ship was built for smuggling, with all sorts of embellishments! In fact, the master was fined more than £500 and there is no doubt that her steward was involved. Next voyage, 200 tons of coal cargo was jettisoned at sea for no apparent reason, causing much speculation amongst her crew! Later, she belonged to de Freitas and Sloman's, both of Hamburg, as the *Nordsee*, but she returned to Norway as the *Fjong*, being broken up in 1925. It will be noted that, unusually for a sailing ship, she has a swinging derrick over No. 2 hatch and, although a steel vessel, she carried a windmill pump which was rigged at intervals. She was a smartly kept and good looking vessel.

369. CRAIGISLA in the Mobile River, Alabama.

Originally built in 1891 on the Tyne by Pickersgills, this vessel was then called the *Verbena* and owned by J. Bell of Liverpool, but later she passed to D. Rose of Aberdeen who, incidentally, owned the famous *Mount Stewart* (Plate 308). Later, like so many good iron ships, she passed to Norway and came into the fleet of E. Monsen of Tvedestrand as the *Craigisla* and in this picture she has her Norwegian neutrality flags painted on her sides. No-one knows how she became lost, for she was posted as missing soon afterwards in 1915.

It may well be thought that Norwegian ships have, perhaps, rather more than their fair share of pictures in this book. If this be true, it is rather an accident of pictures, but the extent of Norwegian ship-owning in the days of sail is seldom appreciated outside that country, any more than it is realised that, in the late 1870's, Canada was the fourth biggest ship-owning country in the world, with nearly 7200 vessels registering 1,333,000 tons. This latter figure may not seem to be much in terms of super-tankers but—and this is the point of much of this book—it was an age of many, small craft.

303

370. BRAMBLETYE coming to anchor.

Flying her numbers as she completes her voyage, the full-rigger *Brambletye* has clewed up all sail save her mizzen upper topsail and mizzen staysail which, centred well abaft her pivotal centre, will throw her head up into the wind quickly as she comes to anchor, reinforcing the effect of the helm. Both sails can be lowered quickly. Built of iron in 1876 for W. P. Price of London, she still had hemp lanyards. Sold to J. Hardie's in 1891, she was scrapped in 1909.

The West Coast of South America was the source of the great saltpetre trade and its anchorage ports were full of square-riggers in the days of sail. Plate 371 shows one of the very last ships to visit Coquimbo—the *Calbuco*, once a lovely iron ship built by A. Stephens as the *Circe* for A. C. Le Quelle of Bordeaux in 1865, which maintained her high standards as the Norwegian *Karmø* from 1903. In 1923 she passed to Oelchers of Chile and became the *Calbuco*, trading on the coast. She lost her mizzen topmast and all the mizzen yards except the crossjack shortly before the war. In 1942 she ran under the Panamanian flag and was scrapped in Savona in 1948.

371. *Seen arriving at Coquimbo, the CALBUCO was neither barque nor full-rigger in her last days.*

372. *Antofagasta in the hey-dey of sail.*

There have been so many beautiful ship forms, but no-one who has seen the Oseberg ship in its museum at Oslo can have left without handing the Norsemen the palm for sheer aesthetic curvature in their shipbuilding. After the Second World War a replica of a Viking longship was built and sailed to England, named the *Huginn*, after one of Odin's ravens. This is an age of replicas, but they have no real value if they are not correct. This particular replica of a *snekkja*, or fighting ship, was well done, and one notes the steering oar to starboard. (*Styr*=steer (board)='starboard'.) We accept that this ship is close to the shore, for Viking ships did not carry shields in the shield rack at sea, despite so many representations to the contrary. It was not only considered to be bad form, but impracticable!

The Viking *knarr*, or round ship, used for trading, was shorter and beamier than the *snekkja* and *skeida*, and known as a 'kaup-ship'. The English would be 'cheaping ship'; the word 'cheaping' meaning 'trading', from which was derived the word 'chapman'—a merchant—and Copenhagen (Kφbenhavn) meaning 'trading har-bour'. (Kaup hamn.)

We have much in our culture from the days of the Danelaw, and a local craft which derives directly from the Vikings is the keel (named from the Saxon word *ceol*) which took its form from the round ship in which the ornamental dragon ends had already become attenuated. Types varied on the Tyne, in the Humber (where they survived the longest) and in the inland waterways, but the fundamentals remained the same. Originally used for loading colliers in the Tyne, vessels there were said to load so many 'keels', the load of a standard keel being $21\frac{1}{5}$ tons=8 chaldrons. With a single square sail (though the inland ones sometimes set a topsail), sweeps or quants were used on occasion, giving rise to the famous North Country ballad *"Weel ma' the keel row"*.

The double-ended hull, clinker-built, was flat-bottomed; the more southern ones being decked forward and aft, with narrow waterways on each side of the large hatch. The stern-post was flush with the deck, to allow working of the tiller. Many were fitted with lee-boards, and the mast was fitted in a tabernacle just forward of the midship point and could be lowered quickly.

306

373. *Replica of a Viking fighting ship—the HUGINN.*

374. *TRIUMPH of Doncaster. Normally there were two rows of reef-points. Some keels could measure 60 x 15 x 6 ft. and could carry 100 tons.*

375. *On the River Trent, near Headley. Viking influence extended right across Europe down to Sicily—(most of the leaders of the first crusade were of Norse stock) and similar sort of craft could be found up the Loire and elsewhere.*

376. Humber keels at Thorne, one under sail.

The Nordlandsbaat, in its various forms, is of the most direct lineage of the Viking craft. Found in North-Western Norway, the Fembøring, with ten oars when being rowed, was used in the Lofoten cod fishery. Usually with a turtle-back cuddy aft, there were two rows of reef-points in the head of the sail and one in the foot, whilst the topsail was set flying. Generally there was a short one-armed yoke attached to the rudder-head, to which the tiller was joined. Thus it needed merely to be worked forward and aft, and not sideways in the more usual manner.

309

377. Fembøring in
     Lofoten.

378. Fembøring homeward bound to
     Lofoten.

379. Ottring, used mainly in the herring fishery, were a smaller form of
     Nordlandsbaat.*
                                                                      *See pp. 286 et seq.

380. Norfolk wherry on the Broads.

If the keel is held to be a first cousin to the Viking round ships, the wherry is sometimes claimed as a second cousin. That she has certain family likenesses is undeniable, but whereas the keel has a tubby hull, the wherry's is graceful, but she is double-ended though does not really seem to have come into existence before Tudor times. Keels had carried many of the passengers locally, and the wherry, possibly deriving her one large fore-and-aft sail from the Dutch, was much handier and faster. She has no bulwarks—to aid quanting—and no lee-boards. Her only standing rigging is the forestay, and her mast is beautifully counterbalanced so that raising and lowering with the high-peaked sail set was no problem. Clinker-built and black-sailed (like the keel), most carried about 25 tons, though some were bigger, and were worked by two men. They seldom anchored, since they could tie up almost anywhere when the wind was foul.

311

381. *ADEONA at Great Yarmouth, with wherry alongside.*

The *Adeona* was one of many craft of her type—a wooden barque of 655 tons built in 1883 in Arendal where she was owned. In 1890, about the time of this picture, Norway owned some 2824 wooden sailing ships—a number which had dropped to 1072 by 1904. The last three were broken up in 1928.

Alongside her is a Norfolk wherry, well loaded and probably going to take a part of the barque's cargo up the waterways to Norwich. These wherries had a good deal of sheer and it will be seen how little freeboard she has amidships. Indeed, when sailing loaded, it was common for the water, even in the narrow, protected rivers, to be swilling right across their waists.

They were particularly adapted for the narrow rivers and the Broads of Norfolk, although they did sometimes sail round to Southwold or Yarmouth. They could point very close to the wind indeed, and made no leeway in the narrow rivers, sailing close to the lee bank, whence the bow wave kept them off.

382. The TALUS badly ashore.

There can be no sorrier sight than a tall ship so out of her element. In this picture we see the *Talus* ashore and right over on the Oregon coast. One of the last of the Golden Fleece line, and retaining their names of Greek mythology, her's was possibly not such a commendable one as those we have already seen (Plates 330 and 331). Talus was, of course, the brass man fabricated by Hephaestus who, whenever he found a stranger on the island, made himself red hot and squeezed him to death. This ship passed from the ownership of Carmichael's to W. Lewis & Co. of Greenock early in the century, and was lost around 1914.

A smart vessel, of 2090 tons gross, she could load 3359 tons or more on occasions, and was built in 1891, with a midship section and flying bridges fore and aft. It is interesting that, having recently built the 4-master *Glaucus*, Carmichael's reverted to a full-rigger when they had the *Talus* laid down. She was known as a good looking ship—hardly apparent in the picture!

313

383. *Remembered latterly as an 'onker' barque in the Thames under the Finnish flag until she went ashore on Norrskarr in 1929 and rolled over and sank, the SHAKESPEARE, built in 1876 of iron in Liverpool for E. C. Friend, spent years afterwards under Norwegian owners, trading all over the world. Here, in Cape Town, she has her neutrality flags on her sides in the First World War.*

384. *While a brigantine gets away ahead of her, this Russian barque squares her mainyards after dropping the pilot. She is unusual in setting a main spencer in addition to a mizzen staysail. Spencers, with notable exceptions (such as Craig's 'Counties') were not used to any great extent, and then usually when reaching or hove-to for stress of weather. This barque, whose name is lost in the limbo of time, looks as though she was built in the Maritime Provinces.*

385. MILTONBURN and DUCHALBURN lying in Santa Rosalia.

Two of Shanklands 'Burn' line—both 'bald-headed', as were so many of their fleet, lie in port with an American schooner. The *Duchalburn* is reputed to have been the first vessel with this ugly, square form of rig, which was also known as the 'jubilee-rig', since it first appeared in 1887, the year of Queen Victoria's jubilee. Some people may be surprised that two vessels of the same company have their hulls painted in different colours, but it was not so unusual.

This volume has barely touched on the great American ship-building effort—their fast, powerful clippers, or the great fleet of wooden vessels built in the states 'Down-east'. The barque on the opposite page was one of the smallest of this spate of building—the *C. D. Bryant*, being 929 tons and built in 1878. No-one would have considered her small a decade or so previously, but comparisons are dictated by current custom and practice, and such terms as 'large' or 'small' must necessarily be used within the context of the type of a vessel and the times in which she existed.

The Down-Easters had a number of distinctive features and were easily recognisable in any port of the world. Moreover, they were exceedingly smart in appearance and, usually, in performance. In this plate the *C. D. Bryant* has lost her main top- and topgallantmasts and fore royal, but she has got herself cleared up and is getting along very nicely.

316

386.   C. D. BRYANT after partial dismasting.

387.   A beautiful iron full-rigger, the LADY ISABELLA, owned by the North British Shipping Co. of Glasgow, wrecked on the Oregon coast.

388. BIG BONANZA.

Built in Newburyport in 1875 for J. Currier Jr., the *Big Bonanza* was of 1475 tons, and was soon bought by San Francisco interests to be operated out of the West Coast of North America. It will be observed that she is about to set her spanker which hoists, as was the case with the vast majority of American square-riggers, whereas the preponderance of European vessels had a standing gaff and a brailing sail. There were no rules about this, and it would almost be possible to produce a book on the variations found in the after-masts of barques, both as regards the form of the spankers and of the gaff topsails. Many vessels set a split gaff topsail, the head of the lower sail stretching in horizontally to the mast from the end of the gaff.* Indeed, inspection of the pictures in this book will show quite a variety of mizzen (or jigger) canvas, but it is by no means comprehensive.

*See Plate 278.

318

389. *PONAPE starting to ship a sea. The long braces were swamped in these conditions.*

390. Changing sail in the Tropics.

When a sailing ship passed through the Tropics she sent down her
good storm sails and bent her oldest suits in their place. This was a
splendid job for the men aloft, but a heavy one for those on deck who
had to wrestle with the long, sausage-like rolls of canvas in the sail-
locker and hump them along the deck.

The scale of the last big sailing ships is seldom appreciated.
Vessels like the *Moshulu*, portrayed here, or the last 'P' 4-masters, had
lower yards weighing over 5 tons, and their circumference was almost
eight feet at the slings (that is, without the sail bent) and just over 3
feet at the yard-arms. They were 95½ feet long and the courses which
were bent to them were 91 feet long and weighed a ton and a half,
being sewn of 00 flax canvas, with double cloths down the buntline
seams. Thus, in the picture of the *Pommern*'s cross-jack being made
fast (Plate 391) the nearest man is ducking to pass the gasket under
the yard to the next man (Alex. Hurst, who has had much to do with
this book), and the man beyond him is doing the same thing to the
next man. The sail is all but stowed.

320

392. *MOSHULU's foresail in Storm—Force 11!*

391. *Making fast the cross-jack.*

393. The big double wheel and twin binnacles of the MAGDALENE VINNEN.

The deep-watermen advanced insofar as their size increased ten-fold in their last half-century of life. Latterly, some had midship sections, which tended to make for dryer and safer decks (though not entirely) and some steered amidships. The long wires needed could accumulate an ugly kick. Much running up and down of ladders was involved when working ship and, in this respect, the long shelter decks were better, but these militated against timber deck cargoes.

One of the most enlightened improvements was Capt. Jarvis' brace winch, (Plate 394) which was a great improvement for trimming yards, though it did not eliminate the use of hand braces altogether. Halliard winches allowed less men (with the same individual effort) to hoist a yard, but they were slow to operate. Equally, ships became equipped with more capstans and cargo winches but, basically, the handling of sails changed scarcely at all and it was here the men were needed. Ships were infinitely stronger aloft, and it was seldom in the last square-riggers that a foresail needed to come in for stress of weather, as in Plate 168, taken in Force 11.

322

395. *Gaff topsails in the 4-masted schooner WESTWARD, ex DANNEFOLK.*

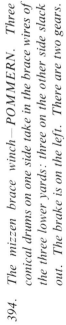

394. *The mizzen brace winch — POMMERN. Three conical drums on one side take in the brace wires of the three lower yards: three on the other side slack out. The brake is on the left. There are two gears.*

396. ELIZABETH of Marstal, off Littlehampton.

Sailing ships were being built after the 1914-1918 war, though there were relatively few. Marstal, in Denmark, produced some smart schooners and barquentines of which the *Elizabeth*, built in 1919 and seen here arriving from the Baltic with a deck cargo of timber, was one. They were distinctive by their spoon bows.

The *Dione*, given a certain enchantment by being framed in the trees of Mariehamn, was built in Åland in 1923 and was one of Gustaf Erikson's lesser-known vessels, being mainly employed in the Baltic trade. She was 182 feet long and 502 tons gross. Erikson bought her in 1934 but, in 1939, she was damaged in collision with a steamer south of Öland and he sold her the next year.

The *Hussar*'s spars seen over a warehouse roof might arouse excitement, yet it is but an illusion. Krupps built this big yacht as a 4-masted barque on a steam yacht's hull in 1931!

398. *Built for Barbara Hutton, the Woolworth heiress, the HUSSAR lies off Dover. She had various changes of name and owner and, perhaps, has no place in this book!*

397. *The bald-headed barquentine DIONE in Mariehamn.*

399.   The stern of the LIBERTAD

Most of the latter-day sailing ship building has been in the form of school-ships and training vessels. Their purpose is utterly different from that of the merchantman. Regrettably, in order to be economically viable, they need to be grossly overmanned and, whilst at a cursory glance at Plate 400, they might give the appearance of a dock a century ago, close inspection (Plate 401) reveals that their decks are a mass of erections: that there is little real working room, and that the old implications of sail-training, as understood, are manifestly impossible. No-one is to blame. It is the March of Time.

The stern of the Argentine *Libertad*, one of the latest of all, has little resemblance to that of a traditional sailing vessel any more than her stockless anchors. Yet, if the deep-water merchant sailing ship was doomed by the steamship and by the canals of Suez and Panama, refusal to abandon tradition hastened her end.

326

400. *School-ships in Oslo's Piperviken. L. to R.:— STATSRAAD LEMKUHL,
DANMARK, MERCATOR, SØRLANDET and GEORG STAGE.*

401. *School-ships lack the open decks of the merchantmen.*

If this volume has only touched on the fringe of merchant sail, which is an enormous subject in its totality, it has illustrated a wide variety of ships and craft. It has not concentrated on the famous vessels unduly, nor on the so-called 'Romance' of sail: on its beauty, its epic tales nor on its hardships. All those things existed in their various degrees, whether in Cape Horners or coasters, flying proas or humble barges. In retrospect, there is much that may be regretted in the passing of these vessels as, indeed, there is much that may be deplored in their conditions in so many instances.

They all had one thing in common. They bred sailors who usually took great pride in their skills. The coaster and fisherman attained skills not given to the Cape Horner, and *vice versa*. In each calling was bred a certain camaradie, character and initiative which was the argument in favour of sail-training ships, as distinct from school-ships in which the purpose is different and in which these attributes cannot automatically be produced.

The 'sailor'—the man of sail as distinct from the seaman—might be ill-equipped to deal with the electronic devices in vast bulk carriers of many thousands of tons deadweight which are propelled through polluted seas with little reck of wind or weather today, and the master in sail would be too bewildered to assist in modern radar-assisted collisions! Yet he understood the run of the sea and the nature of the elements more thoroughly than his modern scientific counterpart. Who knows?—when he has exhausted his fuel resources, man may be forced to consider using merchant sail again.

Many forms of sailing ship could—and should—have been improved in their conditions, in their gear and in their design. Nevertheless, despite this comment, many were perfectly evolved for the conditions in which they found themselves and, whether good or bad, all had a fascination and character which disappeared with them.

The life of their men was undoubtedly harder than that of modern seamen, yet that life provided them with some sense of personal achievement. Like their ships, they, too, are almost all gone. They may have cursed each vessel in which they served, but always there was 'their Last Ship' to be extolled. Ships and men both had their faults but . . . their fascination lingers on!

402. KISMET and THE BROWNIE were two of the last barges left in trade,
but . . .

403. . . . soon they were as much a memory as the sails of the merchant square-riggers.

404. *A small schooner, missing her main topmast and upper topsail—a regular coastal work-horse—passes out of Whitby behind a group of fishermen of her generation. All have passed into history.*